ENCOUNTER

PILOTS IN PERIL!

THE UNTOLD STORY OF U.S. PILOTS
WHO BRAVED "THE HUM

by Steven

Consultant:
John D. Plating
Author of *The Hump: America's Strategy
for Keeping China in World War II*

CAPSTONE PRESS
a capstone imprint

Encounter Books are published by Capstone Press,
1710 Roe Crest Drive, North Mankato, Minnesota 56003
www.capstonepub.com

Library of Congress Cataloging-in-Publication Data
Otfinoski, Steven.
  Pilots in Peril!: The Untold Story of U.S. Pilots Who Braved "The Hump" in World
  War II / by Steven Otfinoski.
    pages cm
    Summary: "Tells the story of U.S. pilots who faced danger every day
    attempting to deliver supplies over "The Hump" to the Chinese during
    World War II"—Provided by publisher.
Includes bibliographical references and index.
ISBN 978-1-4914-5156-4 (library binding); ISBN 978-1-4914-5166-3 (paperback);
ISBN 978-1-4914-5165-6 (ebook PDF); ISBN 978-1-62370-318-9 (paper over board)
1. World War, 1939–1945—Aerial operations, American—Juvenile literature.
2. Airlift, Military—United States—History—20th century—Juvenile literature.
3. United States. Army Air Forces—Airmen—Biography—Juvenile literature.
4. World War, 1939–1945—Himalaya Mountains—Juvenile literature. 5. World War,
1939–1945—China—Juvenile literature. I. Title.

D790.2.O85 2015
940.54'49730922--dc23   2015014234

Editorial Credits

Jennifer Huston, editor; Tracy Davies McCabe, designer;
Jo Miller, media researcher; Tori Abraham, production specialist

Photo Credits

Alamy: Aviation History Collection, 216–217, Avpics, cover, Chronicle, 93, Danita Delimont,
127, Military Images, 68; AP Images, 38, 95, 99; Capstone, 28–29, 143; CBS via Getty Images,
87; Corbis: Bettmann, 102; Getty Images: Keystone, 84, Michael Ochs Archives/Ivan Dmitri,
54, Museum of Science and Industry, Chicago, 48, Time & Life Pictures/William Vandivert, 6;
Newscom: Everett Collection, 24, Everett Collection/CSU Archives, 212; Shutterstock: Dhoxax,
(background), cover, 1, 2–3, 218–232, Hailin Chen, 112–113, 154–155, karinkamon, 40–41, 52–53,
100–101, 206–207, surassawadee, 4–5, 60–61, 194–195, szefei, 131, T photography, 18–19, 72–73,
172–173, Udometer, 214–215, Wouter Tolenaars, 144–145, Zephyr_p, 30–31, 88–89, 124–125,
136–137, 186–187, SuperStock, 116; Toronto Star via Getty Images: Toronto Star Archives, 171;
Wikimedia: Antoine Taveneaux, 43, NARA, 204, U.S. Air Force, 138, Wikimedia/unknown, 33

Printed in the United States of America.
009773F16

TABLE OF
CONTENTS

LOST IN THE
STORM

A U.S. transport plane crosses over "the Hump," a mission that many pilots considered more dangerous than combat.

Private First Class John Huffman wasn't supposed to be on the four-engine C-87 bound for Jorhat, India. But he needed a lift back to his base from Kunming, China, and the four-man crew had no problem letting him hitch a ride on their plane. Like them, Huffman had flown in earlier that last day of November 1943. But he had arrived on another transport plane carrying supplies for the Chinese troops fighting in World War II. Both crews were part of the U.S. Army's "Hump Airlift," risking their lives daily to fly up and over the Himalayan Mountains (the Hump) and into China to deliver food and supplies.

Huffman wasn't a member of this special team. At age 27, he was older than any of the C-87's crew, yet he was the least experienced at flying. He had trained as a flight engineer and was responsible for mechanical operation of the planes. But he had been assigned as a mechanic in the motor pool. Even so, he was curious to see what it was like to fly over the Hump, so he got a ride on a plane earlier that day.

The crew was slightly amused to see how Huffman was dressed. He was wearing a neatly pressed shirt, sharply creased pants, and a heavy sweater under his jacket. He was a nice enough guy, quiet but grateful to get a ride back with them.

IF HE KNEW WHAT LAY AHEAD, HE CERTAINLY WOULD HAVE PUT ASIDE HIS CURIOSITY AND NEVER LEFT JORHAT.

The four crew members were all experienced Hump fliers. Robert Crozier, the pilot, was a friendly and easygoing Texan who was skilled at his job. He had just met his copilot, Harold McCallum, that morning. McCallum had flown fewer missions than Crozier, but he'd known he wanted to be a pilot since he was a boy back in Quincy, Massachusetts. He had strong, handsome features, thick, black hair, and was a bit of a ladies' man.

At age 19, Corporal Kenneth Spencer, the radio operator from Rockville Centre,

New York, was the baby of the bunch. He was tall and thin with freckled skin. In contrast, 22-year-old flight engineer William Perram was built solid with a protruding chin. He hailed from Tulsa, Oklahoma.

To make Huffman feel like part of the team, the crew designated him the assistant engineer. They first made a quick stop at Yunnanyi, 130 miles west of Kunming, where they delivered a small cargo of food. Then it was on to Jorhat. The skies were open and clear. But as Crozier took the plane up to 24,000 feet, that quickly changed. They entered a bank of clouds, and visibility dropped to zero. The temperature began to fall, and ice formed on the wings. It wasn't long after that when the storm hit.

A ROUGH LANDING

It seemed to come out of nowhere, as storms often do in this part of the world. As a strong updraft forced the plane upward, Crozier and McCallum did everything they could to maintain control. Then hurricane-force winds pounded the aircraft, making it difficult for the pilots to keep it from flipping over. But with poor visibility, Crozier was flying blind. They were lost, off course, and unable to determine their direction.

Desperate to find an airfield where they could land, Crozier kept flying until fuel was dangerously low. When two of the engines sputtered and died, the pilot gave the order that no airman ever wants to hear:

"HIT THE SILK."

It was time to bail out or go down with the plane.

The crewmen strapped on their parachutes. But Huffman was in a panic. He had never gotten into a chute before, and he couldn't get it over his bulky clothing. Then to make matters worse, the rear door—out of which they needed to jump—wouldn't open. Crozier, McCallum, and Perram kicked at it wildly, but it wouldn't budge. Finally they removed the pins from the hinges and kicked some more. The door tumbled into the dark void. Just then a third engine gave out.

As the airmen got ready to jump, Huffman was still struggling with his parachute. In a calm voice, McCallum told him to take off his jacket. When he did, he managed to get the chute on, but he couldn't fasten the buckle on his harness. Then the last engine sputtered and died. There was no time to waste. Finally, just in the nick of time, the buckle on Huffman's harness clicked. He followed Crozier and Spencer out the gaping hole in the plane. McCallum and Perram followed close behind.

DOWN, DOWN, DOWN THEY FLOATED, SWINGING TO AND FRO IN THE DARKNESS.

As Huffman tumbled to the ground, he rolled into a rock and was knocked unconscious. When he came to, he found himself wedged in a crevice in a mountainside. His nose was bleeding, and there was a deep cut over his left eye. Worst of all, searing pains in his left shoulder told him it was likely broken.

Huffman pulled his parachute around him like a blanket to fight off the subzero temperatures. He stayed that way until he heard voices at daybreak. He cried out to

them, but they didn't hear him. He yelled
until he was hoarse but got no answer.
Then suddenly, the voices were gone.

**HE WAS LOST IN THE WILDERNESS
ALL ALONE. IN WHAT BARREN PLACE
HAD THEY LANDED?**

Realizing that he could count on no one
to help him, Huffman pulled the jungle
knife from his survival kit and cut a strip
of silk from his parachute. He made a
crude sling from it for his left arm. Next he
discarded the heavy over-boots he had worn
over his shoes on the plane and began the
long, painful descent from the mountain to
the valley below. It took him seven hours.

While making his way down the
mountain, he saw the footprints of three
men—undoubtedly his comrades—so he
followed them. He trudged alongside a

river for nine more hours until, utterly exhausted, he found a sheltered place to sleep for the night.

If Huffman was in a tight spot, Perram was in an even tighter one. He had landed alone on the far side of the mountain, his leg injured in the landing. Unsure which way to go, he wasted precious time in indecision. When he finally started to climb farther up the mountain to get a view of his surroundings, it took him much longer than he expected. His breathing was labored in the thin mountain air, and it was difficult crossing the rugged, rocky ground. Once he made it atop the mountain, he couldn't find another route back down. He would have to spend a second frigid night outdoors.

While their crewmates were struggling to stay alive, Crozier and Spencer descended to the river and linked up with McCallum on a sandbank. In sharp contrast to the mountain, the valley was dry and hot. As they hiked along the riverbank, a warm wind blew dust and dirt into their faces, stinging their eyes.

AFTER A FULL DAY OF WALKING, THEY CAME TO THE BITTER REALIZATION THAT THEY WERE GOING IN THE WRONG DIRECTION.

They had been heading east instead of their intended western route, which they hoped would eventually take them toward their base in India. Of course, they had no way of knowing if they were already in India or if they were still in China.

VILLAGE OF FEAR

On the morning of December 2, Crozier, Spencer, and McCallum retraced their steps along the river. That afternoon they spotted a caravan of men and animals in the distance. They followed the caravan at a safe distance until they saw it enter a village. Would the villagers be friendly? There was no way of knowing, but the airmen decided to risk it and entered the village. What other choice did they have? How could they keep going without food or fresh water?

Immediately there were distressing signs. Some of the huts were decorated with what appeared to be swastikas, the emblem of the enemy, Nazi Germany. A group of villagers appeared and stared at them. But these were not friendly stares. Some of the men had sharp knives on their belts.

More villagers gathered to gawk as the men walked through the growing crowd. When someone reached out and grabbed at one of them, McCallum pulled out his pistol and fired into the air. The crowd fell back in fear.

The airmen decided it was time to get out of there. They turned and began moving quickly alongside the river. But they could hear angry muttering behind them. The crowd was in pursuit. The Americans could not outrun the villagers. If they were to die in this horrible place, at least they would die as soldiers, fighting to the end. They stopped and turned, taking their stand. The airmen drew their pistols as the crowd closed in.

CHAPTER 2

BIRTH OF
THE HUMP

What brought the five young Americans halfway around the world to a tiny village in the Himalayas? The answer lies far back in history, long before the world war that America found itself fighting. For centuries, China and Japan were the two great powers of the Far East. By the late 1800s, Japan was the stronger of the two. Japan desired more land for its growing population and dreamed of an empire on the mainland. Meanwhile China, which was once a mighty kingdom, had been weakened by civil war and political corruption. Then in 1894 Japan and China went to war over Korea, a nation that had been under China's control for centuries. Japan won the war within a year, and Korea quickly came under Japanese influence. The Japanese also seized the Chinese island of Taiwan.

China's last ruling dynasty collapsed in 1911. Two decades later, Japan's military leaders seized Manchuria, a region in northern China. They turned it into a puppet state from which they could attack other parts of northern China. By 1938 Japanese forces occupied China's eastern seaboard. They destroyed China's navy and air force and cut off its major ports from trade with Western nations. This greatly troubled the United States, which sent military aid and advisers to China to keep the Japanese away. Despite the American support, the Japanese drove the Nationalist Chinese government into the province of Szechwan. The Nationalists were led by General Chiang Kai-shek. They were in conflict with the Chinese Communists, who were led by Mao Zedong. At times, the Nationalist government was fighting both Japan and Communist China.

Japanese aggression in Asia was mirrored in Europe by Nazi Germany. In September 1939 Nazi leader Adolf Hitler invaded Poland. Soon after, Great Britain, France, and their allies declared war on Germany.

WORLD WAR II HAD OFFICIALLY BEGUN.

The United States tried to remain neutral in the war, but that ended on December 7, 1941. On that clear Sunday morning, the Japanese launched a surprise attack on the U.S. naval fleet stationed at Pearl Harbor in Hawaii. Several ships and more than 320 aircraft were damaged or destroyed and nearly 2,400 soldiers and civilians were killed. The next day the United States declared war on Japan. Soon after, the United States joined the rest of the

Allies in their fight against Germany, Italy, and the other Axis powers.

The United States hoped to prevent China from falling to Japan, which would be devastating to the Allies. Realizing this, U.S. President Franklin D. Roosevelt agreed to supply the Chinese with weapons, vehicles, ammunition, gasoline, machinery, and medical supplies. Keeping China in the war would tie up about a third of all Japanese troops. That, in turn, would keep them from fighting American troops in the Pacific.

A ROUTE IN THE SKY

American supplies and troops flowed along the only ground route that remained open to China—the Burma Road. At about 715 miles long, this twisty, gravel road went from Burma (now called Myanmar), to Kunming, China. But in early 1942,

A section of the Burma Road in Annan, China, is famous for its dizzying 21 curves.

Japan seized much of Burma and closed the Burma Road. If the crucial delivery of supplies to China was to continue, a new route would have to be found.

The only land route lay from northeastern India through the mountainous nation of Tibet. But a road there did not exist and creating one would be impossible. Instead, U.S. military commanders came up with an alternative. The goods would be shipped from the United States to Bombay in western India or Karachi (now in eastern Pakistan). They would then travel by train to the Assam province in northeastern India. From there they would fly more than 500 miles to Kunming in southern China. The only problem was that they would have to fly over the 15,000-foot-high Santsung Range of the Himalayas on the way to China.

THE WORLD HAD NEVER SEEN SUCH A LARGE AND COMPLEX SUPPLY CHAIN.

Initially the Hump airlift was run by the United States' Assam-Burma-China (ABC) Command and was part of the 10th Air Force. In April 1942 Brigadier General Donald Old, commander of the 10th Air Force, piloted the first Hump flight. He was part of a convoy that carried 30,000 gallons of gasoline and 500 pounds of oil. Ten days later 26 crews of American soldiers and pilots began the long journey from the United States to India in C-47 transport planes.

The ABC Command crews were not enthusiastic about their mission to China. These pilots considered themselves combat fliers, so they felt that flying cargo, no matter how necessary and important, was beneath them. During the summer of 1942, the cargo they flew averaged about 700 tons a month—not an impressive amount.

On December 1, 1942, the Air Transport Command (ATC), a newly created unit of the Air Force, took over the Hump route. The combat pilots of the 10th sarcastically said the acronym really stood for "Allergic to Combat" and referred to the Hump airmen as no more than "aerial truck drivers."

But that opinion would change as the operation grew. Hump crews flew what was soon recognized as one of the most hazardous air routes in any theater of the war. Beginning in late 1943, they did it 24 hours a day, day in and day out. Overall the conditions in the China-Burma-India (CBI) theater were seen as the most dangerous, both in the air and on the ground.

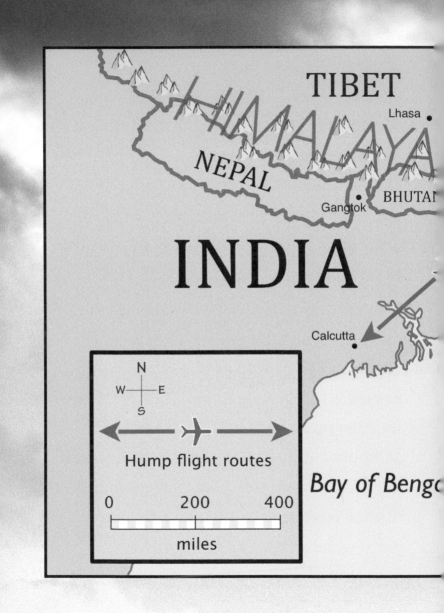

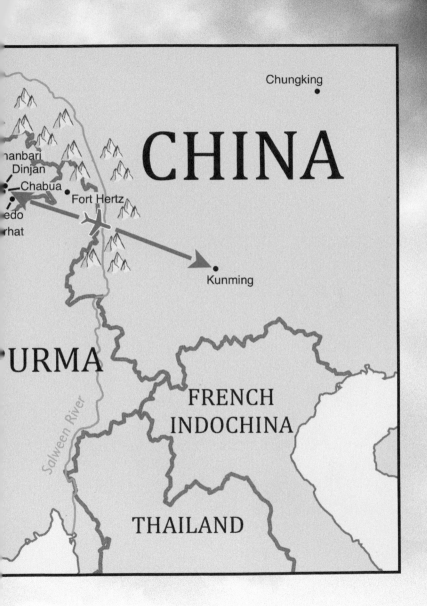

CHAPTER 3

STRANGERS IN A STRANGE LAND

As the crowd closed in on them, Crozier, Spencer, and McCallum stood still with their pistols drawn. Suddenly a man in a thick fur coat stepped forward from the crowd. He approached the Americans, put his hands together, and touched them to his forehead. "As salaam alaikum," he said.

McCallum knew some Hindustani, one of the most widely-spoken languages of India. He knew the greeting meant "Peace be with you."

"ALAIKUM AS SALAAM," HE REPLIED, WHICH MEANS "AND PEACE WITH YOU."

McCallum asked him if they were in India. The man shook his head. "Tibet," he said pointing to the ground.

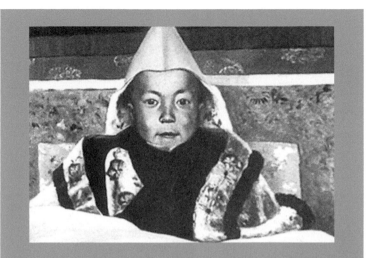

TIBET—A LAND WHERE TIME STOOD STILL

Tibet is a remote, ancient kingdom that stretches from India to China. Home to the Himalayas, the highest mountain chain on Earth, Tibet has rightfully been called "The Roof of the World." At the time that the Hump airmen arrived, life there had changed very little since the Middle Ages.

The supreme ruler of Tibet is the Dalai Lama, a high Buddhist priest. Tibetans believe that each Dalai Lama is the reborn soul of the one who ruled before him. Using what they believe to be heavenly clues, they search among the children of their country for the next Dalai Lama. When the airmen arrived in Tibet, the present Dalai Lama was only 8 years old.

GUESTS AND PRISONERS

The man's name was Sona Ullah, and, unlike nearly all Tibetans, he had traveled outside his country to India as a trader. He explained that the people of this village, called Tsetang, meant no harm. They were simply curious about the strangers because very few Westerners had ever set foot in Tibet. The Americans also learned that what they thought were swastikas were not connected to the Nazis. They were actually ancient symbols used in the Buddhist religion.

Ullah invited the Americans to his house, a two-story dwelling with mud-brick walls. There were no stairs, so they climbed a ladder to reach the second story. The villagers' curiosity about the visitors was intense. They crowded into Ullah's house as he translated McCallum's story of how the airmen had dropped out of the sky. After the last group left, Ullah fed his guests a stew and a greasy, yellow tea that tasted awful to the Americans. But they forced it down so as not to offend their host.

The next day McCallum told the village elders about their two lost comrades. The elders agreed to organize a search party but would not let the airmen accompany it.

ALTHOUGH THE AMERICANS WERE TREATED WELL, THEY WERE BASICALLY PRISONERS OF THE TIBETANS. THEY WOULD SOON LEARN WHY.

When the search party returned two days later, they brought bad news. They told the three airmen that Huffman and Perram were dead.

STRANDED IN THE WILDERNESS

Actually, both men were very much alive. The Tibetans probably wanted to cover up the fact that they had failed to find them. After three days of walking, Huffman had reached a village. His arm was still in a sling and dried blood from other injuries covered his face and hair. The villagers greeted him and fed him, and the next day he was guided to another village. There, two men handed him a note from McCallum, which said the others were in Tsetang. Late on the following day, an exhausted Huffman stumbled into Tsetang and was joyfully reunited with his crewmates.

Perram hobbled in a few hours later, his feet numb with frostbite from prolonged exposure in the freezing temperatures. The men were happy to be together again.

**THEY WERE LUCKY TO BE ALIVE
BUT DID NOT REALIZE
THE DELICATE POLITICAL SITUATION
THEY HAD STUMBLED INTO.**

Since the 1700s, China had controlled Tibet, but that changed after the fall of the Qing Dynasty in October 1911. In 1913, the Dalai Lama declared that Tibet was an independent nation. But once World War II was underway, Tibet was again threatened by China.

Strangers were rare in this remote land and were looked upon with suspicion. Word of the Americans' arrival had reached the government in Lhasa, the capital. Government officials feared that the strangers were spies for the Chinese. This belief was supported by the fact that one of the airmen had a Chinese flag sewn on his leather jacket. In reality, the flag was a

American airmen flying over the Hump wore leather jackets with the Chinese flag sewn on them. This identified the airmen as Americans and friendly to the Chinese.

signal to the Chinese that the airman was an American—an ally that needed help.

Word finally came from Lhasa that the Americans were to be brought there for questioning. In their remaining time in Tsetang, the airmen continued to be a source of curiosity for the Tibetans.

**PEOPLE FROM OTHER VILLAGES
CAME TO STARE AT THEM FOR HOURS
LIKE VISITORS GAWKING AT
CAGED ANIMALS IN A ZOO.**

A group of officials finally arrived from the capital several days later to escort the Americans to Lhasa. Accompanied by Ullah and the officials, the Americans departed on mules the following morning. Crozier's mule was so small that both his feet could touch the ground as he rode. To the men's surprise, they passed the burnt shell of their plane.

Each crewman took a piece of the plane as a souvenir and then moved on. The local Tibetans would carve up the rest of the plane and use the parts for tools.

4

TO TIBET AND BACK

The trek to Lhasa would not be an easy one. They had to get over a 19,000-foot-mountain at Gokar-la, one of the highest mountain passes in the world. Unaccustomed to the thin air at that altitude, the airmen suffered severe headaches and nausea. Perram's toes were better, but he was still unable to walk.

IN THE FORBIDDEN CITY

On December 15, after several days of traveling, the airmen and their escorts arrived on the outskirts of Lhasa, the "Forbidden City." Only a handful of Americans had seen it before them. The airmen gazed in awe at the Potala Palace— the winter home of the Dalai Lama. The palace was crowned by gold canopies atop the rocky heights, where the tombs of past Dalai Lamas resided.

The Potala Palace sits at the top of Red Mountain, which rises about 12,000 feet above sea level.

The Americans received a warm welcome even before they entered the city. They were taken to a tent where they met Dr. Kung Chin-tsung, the Chinese representative in Tibet. There they sat on cushions and were treated to a rich selection of food and drink. Dr. Kung wanted to impress the Americans and gain their trust and support before the Tibetans got to them.

But the citizens of Lhasa had a very different welcome for the airmen. That evening as they made their way to a banquet hosted by Dr. Kung, a crowd of people shouted angry words. Spencer was struck in the head by a flying rock. Then McCallum was hit on the shoulder with a clump of dirt.

Tibetan police forced back the crowd as the Americans fled on their mules.

Later that night, George Sherriff, head of the British mission in Tibet, welcomed them to his luxurious home on the other side of Lhasa. For the first time since they left their base in Jorhat, the men slept in real beds with soft mattresses.

BUT THEIR TROUBLES WERE FAR FROM OVER.

Soon after the arrival of the Americans, a trio of government officials, dressed in brightly colored robes, showed up to question them. They quickly came to the same conclusion that Sherriff did—that the airmen were not spies but had entered Tibet purely by accident. The officials decided that the airmen could return to India as soon as Perram and Huffman had sufficiently recovered from their injuries. But as the days passed, the men grew anxious.

WINTER WAS SETTING IN, AND IF THEY DIDN'T LEAVE SOON, THEY MIGHT NOT GET THROUGH THE SNOW-COVERED MOUNTAIN PASSES UNTIL SPRING.

While attending a party that Sherriff held in their honor, the Americans were told that they could leave the following morning. Sherriff managed to get a day's extension for them. Before they left, they were given special passports that would get them food and lodging at any village along the way.

They said goodbye to Ullah and paid him generously for his services.

On December 19, 1943, just four days after arriving in Lhasa, the Americans left the Forbidden City. They were accompanied by a guide, two Tibetan soldiers, and a cook they nicknamed Duncan Hines, after the famous American food writer. Ahead they faced 400 miles of rough terrain before reaching their destination of Gangtok, in the Indian state of Sikkim. Higher and higher they climbed on their little mules to the first major mountain pass at Nyapso La. During this first part of the journey, Crozier suffered from acute mountain sickness (AMS) from the oxygen-depleted air. This disease causes dizziness, headaches, nausea, and shortness of breath. Crozier was so dizzy and weak that he could barely stay on his mule. The others experienced nosebleeds and pounding headaches due to the thin, mountain air. After reaching the pass at Nyapso La, they started back down a narrow trail through a gorge.

WHEN CROZIER'S MULE SLIPPED, THE AIRMAN WAS THROWN AND WENT TUMBLING OVER A CLIFF.

The only thing that saved him from certain death was that his shoulder became wedged between two rocks. His comrades tossed him a rope, but Crozier was too weak to pull himself up. Spencer and McCallum went down and lifted him to safety.

They soon reached the town of Gyantse. Two British officers stationed there greeted them and invited them to their evening festivities. The Americans had completely forgotten that it was Christmas Eve.

Robert Crozier and his crew were flying a C-87 transport plane like the one seen here over the Hump when their aircraft went down in Tibet.

THEY WERE SO EXHAUSTED THAT DURING DINNER, MCCALLUM FELL ASLEEP AND HIS HEAD DROPPED INTO HIS BOWL OF SOUP.

When Huffman and Perram became ill, the travelers had to postpone their journey. Finally, on New Year's Eve, they trudged on toward Sikkim. Four days later, they had only 12 miles left to go. They figured they could make it to Sikkim before nightfall, but then it started to snow. Visibility was reduced nearly to zero as fat flakes fell like confetti. Soon they were up to their knees in the white stuff. By the following morning, the snow was waist deep. If it weren't for the mules and the hearty Tibetans urging them on, the Americans wouldn't have made it to Sikkim.

IN THE HOME STRETCH

As they neared the Tibet-Sikkim border, their Tibetan companions (except for Duncan Hines) bid them farewell. The Americans were sorry to see them go. They had come to appreciate these warm, loyal, and courageous people. As they descended to ground level, an excited McCallum fired his pistol to announce their arrival in India.

SUDDENLY THE EARTH SHOOK AND WHAT SOUNDED LIKE THUNDER ROARED ACROSS THE SKY.

It sounded like a freight train was coming toward them as an avalanche rumbled down the mountainside, just barely missing them. McCallum wiped the sweat from his brow and put away his pistol. There'd be no more shooting that day.

Upon their arrival at Gangtok, the British official said to the ragtag group of Americans, "I trust you had a good trip?" They didn't know whether to laugh or cry.

From Gangtok they caught a ride on a mail truck and then took a train to Calcutta. They finally arrived back at the American base in Jorhat on January 20, 1944. What began as a five-hour flight had taken nearly two months and had brought them to a place that few outsiders had ever seen.

THE ALUMINUM TRAIL

The air route from India to China had another nickname besides the Hump—"The Aluminum Trail." Because the route was relatively short, the wreckage of the many planes that went down along it was easily visible from the sky. The path of this wreckage came to be called the Aluminum Trail because aluminum was the main material of these downed planes. Pilots said they could follow the
route just by following the twisted path of wrecked aircraft below.

Chick Marrs Quinn, whose husband died when his plane went down over the Hump on February 27, 1945, published a book called *The Aluminum Trail*. Her book listed every lost plane, where it went down, and the airmen on it. Few copies of *The Aluminum Trail* still exist, but it remains the go-to book for individuals who continue to search for missing Hump airmen.

DAREDEVIL PILOTS, PROBLEMATIC PLANES

Many of the planes flown over the Hump experienced mechanical problems. Soldiers at the base in Assam, India, worked to fix them.

The courageous crew members who were stranded in Tibet were typical examples of the Hump airmen. They were young, mostly in their early to mid-twenties. They came from varied backgrounds—rural communities, small towns, and large cities. Some dropped out of college to enlist in the war. Few had much military or flying experience before they enlisted.

PROBLEMS AT THE BASE

What is perhaps most surprising about the brave Hump airmen is that many of them received little or no training. Morale was also a problem on the Hump bases almost from the beginning. The food was bad and the stores on base often lacked everyday items such as candy, magazines, and razor blades. There were also few recreational activities available except for reading, talking, and playing cards.

Although crew members were polite to each other, there were few lasting friendships. There were two reasons for this. First, death in the air came without warning.

YOU COULD SEE A FELLOW PILOT AT BREAKFAST AND GET THE WORD AT DINNERTIME THAT HE WAS AMONG THE MISSING OR DEAD.

The emotional toll was too great, so airmen kept some distance from one another to avoid getting too close. Second, there were no set flight crews. The constant scheduling of flights may have made this a necessity, but it didn't build confidence among crewmates. They often met for the first time shortly before takeoff.

Yet for all these problems, a certain sense of unity developed among the airmen. Flight crews challenged each other to see who could fly the most tonnage in a day. They also competed to see who would first meet the goal of 650 flight hours required to be sent back home.

To break the boredom of base life, pilots played practical jokes on each other. New recruits, especially copilots, were often the butt of these jokes. During flights rookies were asked to look for a secret passageway across the Himalayas that, of course, didn't exist.

One member of a search-and-rescue squadron got into bed one night to find that a pilot had cut off the bed's legs. Later the pilot who shortened the bed climbed into his own to find a goose squawking next to him.

THE LONGER THEY SPENT ON THE HUMP, THE MORE REBELLIOUS AND RESISTANT TO RULES THE AIRMEN BECAME.

Some grew mustaches and beards, which went against military policy. Others didn't bathe regularly, and some even stopped saluting officers.

UNRELIABLE AIRCRAFT

The aircraft the airmen flew were individuals too. You never knew when you went up in a plane how it would perform.

Hump airmen flew several different kinds of aircraft. But the most popular was the C-46, a bulky transport plane, which initially had all sorts of technical problems. Its engines could fail without warning, its carburetor tended to ice up in the Hump's freezing temperatures, and hydraulic fluid often leaked. The planes were frequently loaded beyond their capacity, and this caused pilots concern. Many crews had to dump cargo while in the air to gain enough altitude to rise above an approaching mountain. The lighter the aircraft, the easier it could rise and more quickly avoid Japanese fighter planes.

Some planes were faulty because they were old and in poor shape. But some new models were sent to bases before the bugs had been worked out. For example, 30 new C-46s were so unreliable that they were flown back to the factory for necessary repairs.

Once in service, planes were kept running constantly and, like the men who flew them, they too got little rest. Regular maintenance was difficult to receive at remote airstrips, and spare parts for repairs were often hard to come by.

THERE WERE TIMES WHEN LESS THAN HALF THE AIRPLANES AT A BASE WERE IN FLYING CONDITION.

Yet the majority of planes held up surprisingly well given the stress and conditions. Like the pilots and crew who flew them day and night, they were tough survivors.

HUNG UP IN THE JUNGLE

Bailing out of a plane is always a stressful situation. It is even more intense when the person in the parachute is leaping into the unknown. Who knows where he might land—on a mountaintop, a pile of rocks, the hard ground, or in a tree. This last spot was where James C. Cooper ended up when he bailed out of his plane on February 7, 1944. It was an experience he'd never forget and one he almost didn't live to tell about.

LOST IN THE CLOUDS

Heading back to home base in Mohanbari, India, copilot Cooper's C-46 transport plane left Kunming around 2:00 a.m. Pilot Roscoe Smith and radio operator John Hillkirk were also on board. Broken clouds slowly gave way to an overcast sky. Smith did his best to find an airport—any airport—in the Assam Valley. But his efforts were all in vain. They had completely lost their bearings. After five hours in the air, the men had no idea where they were. By then it was morning, but they could only see thin slivers of land through the solid bank of clouds. The airmen had about 15 minutes before the plane would run out of fuel. There was no option but to jump. Down below, through an opening in the clouds, the airmen could see a village atop a hill in the Burmese jungle. They decided to jump within close range of it and hope that the villagers were friendly.

COOPER BAILED OUT FIRST. HIS PARACHUTE POPPED OPEN WITH A SWOOSH, AND HE GENTLY ROCKED BACK AND FORTH AS HE SAILED DOWNWARD.

He landed on a large limb of a tall tree, but it wasn't a lucky landing. He was too high up in the tree to safely climb down.

The next nearest branch was 20 feet below him. If he jumped for it, chances were good that he'd miss it and plunge 200 feet to certain death. There was nothing he could do but hang there helplessly and wait. But would his buddies ever see him high up in the leafy tree? He pulled out his gun and fired into the air three times. Surely if Smith and Hillkirk had landed safely they would hear the shots and come looking for him. But the only sound he heard was the wind rustling in the trees.

TRAPPED IN A TREE

The seriousness of Cooper's situation began to sink in. Tangled in his parachute, he was unable to reach his survival kit, which contained his only food. How long could he last without food and drink suspended like a fly in a spider's web?

He'd heard stories about airmen in similar situations who had turned their pistols on themselves rather than face a slow, lingering death.

HE DIDN'T WANT TO THINK ABOUT THAT, BUT HE DECIDED TO KEEP ONE BULLET IN RESERVE—JUST IN CASE.

Minutes passed. Then an hour. Then two and three. After four hours, as he was starting to worry that he'd never get out of the tree alive, Cooper heard voices. They weren't speaking English but some strange language he didn't recognize. He looked down and saw small, muscular men squatting around the tree. They were talking excitedly and glanced up every so often at him. After a while, they got up and went to work. Some cut down limbs with their large, flat-bladed knives, while others began to climb the tree.

Cooper told himself that they had to be friendly. If not, why would they be coming to get him down?

COULD THEY BE HEADHUNTERS, COMING TO RESCUE HIM ONLY TO MOUNT ANOTHER TROPHY ON THE WALL OF A HUT?

The climbers drew closer, chopping off branches and vines with quick, skillful motions. For a moment, Cooper feared that they would cut the limbs holding his parachute, but then he realized that they had a plan to get him down safely.

They passed forked branches to him and directed him to place them into the limb above him. Then they had him tie the lower part of the branches to the harness with a sturdy vine. Placing several of the limbs in a vertical line would prevent the parachute from falling as he moved downward.

One tribesman tossed a long vine to Cooper and gestured for him to tie it around his harness.

AT THAT MOMENT COOPER NOTICED AN ARMY OF RED ANTS, EACH ABOUT THREE-QUARTERS OF AN INCH LONG. THEY WERE MARCHING ACROSS THE HARNESS AND CRAWLING ALL OVER HIM.

He tried to beat them off, but there too many of them, and he was bitten repeatedly. The natives urged him to move faster down the vine. After making his way down to a lower limb, two natives grabbed him. Cooper was then able to slowly lower himself safely down the tree to the ground.

The natives—who were members of the Kachin tribe—looked fierce. The older men had tattoos on their faces and torsos and carried long knives and spears tipped with steel spikes.

Parachutes often got tangled up in trees when airmen bailed out over the jungle. Like James Cooper, this airman needed some help getting down from a tree.

But they treated him like a friend. They gave him cooked rice wrapped in banana leaves and then took him to their village, named Aonbow. This was the village he had seen from the plane. He was elated to see Smith and Hillkirk were also there, having landed only a half mile from each other.

As they talked, a group of tribesmen entered the village with baskets filled with bits of metal and plastic on their backs. The airmen suddenly realized that the Kachins had found their downed plane and had stripped whatever they could from it. They would transform these bits of metal into usable tools and weapons.

The next day, the village chieftain took the three men to a place nearby where English and American soldiers were stationed. From there, they sent news of their bailout and a request for food and supplies. On the way back, they went by their plane, which was nearly stripped clean by the natives. They returned to the village, tired and discouraged.

SEVERAL DAYS PASSED WITH NO COMMUNICATION FROM THE OUTSIDE WORLD.

Finally, after nearly a week, a C-47 dropped packages of food and other supplies. They were told that natives nearby were carving out space for a tiny airfield where a small plane could land. After they arrived there, it took about two more weeks to finish the airstrip.

On March 14, 1944, a single-engine L-1 plane came down for a landing, but it only had room for two passengers. Smith and Cooper took off in the plane, and the pilot returned to pick up Hillkirk the next day. On its return to the small airfield, the plane made a crash landing. Hillkirk had to wait another day to be lifted out of the jungle. But soon all three men were back at their base in Assam. They were grateful for the help of the Kachin natives, none more so than James Cooper, who thought he might never make it down from that 200-foot tree.

CHAPTER 7

POLITICIANS, CHINESE COLONELS, AND A WAR CORRESPONDENT

A damaged carburetor or a dying engine plays no favorites. Neither high-ranking officers nor ordinary airmen and their passengers were immune to danger on the Hump. This was dramatically proven on August 2, 1943. On that day a twin-engine C-46 left Chabua, India, for Kunming with four crew members and 17 passengers.

State Department official John Paton Davies was among the passengers. CBS news correspondent Eric Sevareid and William T. Stanton of the Board of Economic Warfare were also on board. Sevareid was on his way to Kunming to interview General Chennault, head of the 14th Air Force. Davies and Stanton were continuing on to the U.S. embassy in Chungking.

The new C-46s had plenty of problems. In fact, six of them had already crashed on the Hump. An official order had banned nonmilitary passengers from flying on them. The notable passengers on this particular flight had talked the flight officer into ignoring the order. In a short time, they would regret that decision.

THE AIRCRAFT HAD BEEN IN THE AIR ONLY ABOUT AN HOUR WHEN ONE OF ITS TWO ENGINES SEIZED.

Pilot Harry Nevue knew they wouldn't make it over the Hump with just one engine. He had no choice but to order the crew to dump the passengers' baggage overboard. They watched in shock as their belongings were tossed into the sky to lighten the load. None were more regretful than Sevareid, who watched his typewriter and briefcase hurled into the wild blue yonder. But soon the problem of losing their belongings would be the least of their worries.

INTO THE JUNGLE

When the second engine began to fail, the plane made a rapid descent. In minutes it would crash. The passengers strapped on their parachutes, stunned by the sudden seriousness of their situation. Davies leaped out the hatch first, but the others huddled about indecisively. Stanton elbowed his way through the crowd crying,

"FOR GOD'S SAKE GET OUT OF THE WAY IF YOU AREN'T GOING TO JUMP."

As he leaped from the plane, his words and actions motivated the others. Sevareid tumbled headfirst on his way down, convinced he was going to fall to his death. When his parachute finally popped open, he thought to himself,

"MY GOD, I'M GOING TO LIVE."

But when he saw the burning wreckage of the crashed plane below, he worried that he would land on it and die. However, the wind blew him clear of the wreckage, and he landed in high jungle grass.

There he met up with two other passengers who had also landed uninjured. A third man, flight radio operator Walter Oswalt, was lying on the ground with an injured ankle. Pilot Nevue was also nearby. He suffered a cracked rib in the bailout.

A welcoming committee of Naga tribesman came out of the leafy jungle to greet the men. Despite their tattooed bodies and the weapons they wielded, these tribesmen of northern Burma were friendly and eager to help. They knew that their efforts would be rewarded with food and other supplies dropped from the sky by the Americans. The tribesmen led the airmen to their village, called Pangsha, which was about a mile away. They carried Oswalt on a litter or a stretcher made of bamboo.

From there the men were taken to a large hut that would be their home for the days to come. Everyone but copilot Charles Felix and Corporal Basil Lemmon was safely accounted for. Lemmon was eventually found alive, but Felix's body was later discovered at the crash site. He had jumped from the plane too late, and his parachute had gotten tangled in the aircraft's tail, dragging him down with it.

A search plane quickly spotted the survivors and returned later with flight surgeon Don Flickinger and two assistants. They parachuted down into the village to provide medical aid.

TENSION WITH THEIR HOSTS

The hospitality of the Nagas, however, could not be taken for granted. They were a warlike people and if their mood changed, it could be dangerous for the Americans. Although the chief appreciated the supplies dropped from the airplane, he feared the packages would crush their crops. He told the airmen they should move away from the village, which they were happy to do.

The Nagas built them three huts about a third of a mile from Pangsha.

While they awaited rescue, the men adapted to their new homes. Each one had specific duties to fulfill. Stanton was in charge of signaling to the search planes. Robert Lee, one of two Chinese-American officers, and Sergeant Francis Signor were in charge of gathering the packages that the planes dropped. The Chinese officers helped with meals by cooking Chinese rice, a camp favorite. Sevareid did double duty as the group's historian and chaplain, a role he felt awkward filling but was well suited for. He conducted a short religious service each Sunday morning.

To keep the men active and their morale from sinking, Flickinger led them in a strict routine of exercises twice a day. They even conducted a mini-Olympics that featured events such as the broad jump, running, and, for the Nagas' sake, spear-throwing.

Despite the activity, the men grew restless and discouraged. It was monsoon season, which brought very heavy rainfall. Their huts were topped with palm leaves, which leaked heavily during the persistent rains. They were also tormented by fleas, which infested their bed mats and everything else in the huts.

Help finally arrived about two weeks into their stay at Pangsha.

"OUT OF THE MIST OF THE JUNGLE A TALL YOUNG MAN [APPEARED] WEARING A HALO OF SHINING FAIR HAIR ... A SOFT BLUE POLO SHIRT ... [AND] BLUE SHORTS," SEVAREID REPORTED. "HE WAS PHILIP ADAMS, THE SAHIB OF MOKOKCHUNG [A TOWN IN NORTHERN BURMA], KING OF THESE DARK AND SAVAGE HILLS."

Adams, a British official, was accompanied by an armed escort and about 50 native bearers, who carried food and other supplies. Adams had received news that neighboring natives might attack the Americans. As a result, he and his group covered 85 miles in five days to reach them.

ADAMS' QUIET AIR OF AUTHORITY AND HIS PROTECTIVE GUARD GAVE NEW HOPE TO THE SURVIVORS.

Preparations were made at once to move out and get the men back to India. But as the hours passed, tensions rose between the native bearers and the local villagers. The bearers were annoyed that the locals would be left with all the remaining food and supplies in the parapacks, when they had done all the work to get Adams there. They took their anger out on the Americans, for whom the packs had been dropped. At one point, the bearers drew their swords, and it looked like the Americans would have a difficult fight on their hands. But Adams never lost his cool. He placed the packs under the guard of the armed escort. Then he turned all the supplies over to the local chieftains to distribute as they saw fit. Tensions lessened, and the party prepared to leave the village.

THE LONG MARCH BACK

The large group stretched out in a column about 2 miles long. They hiked along the twisting trails by day and stayed in a different village each night. Soon they were climbing mountains, with the sure-footed Nagas pulling the men to the mountaintops with long vines. By August 21, four days after leaving Pangsha, the exhausted airmen had reached their breaking point. For three

John Davies, William Stanton, and Eric Sevareid (left to right) survived in the jungle for nearly a month after bailing out of a plane in northern Burma.

hours, they toiled up a mountainside, using native spears for hiking sticks. Despite their own exhaustion, Flickinger and the medics treated a host of ailments, including sunstroke, sore feet, insect bites, fevers, and sprains. At one point, Sevareid fell down in the rain and muck and broke the spear that he was hoping to bring back as a souvenir. Looking back on the tiresome trek, the newsman recalled,

"I COULD NOT DO IT AGAIN."

On August 23 they finally reached Mokokchung, a large settlement about 40 miles into the Naga Hills. There Sevareid sent a report on their ordeal to his network. Then the trek resumed. Finally on August 28, the group was met by men in army trucks and jeeps. They had been sent to take the men to an airfield 40 miles away. There, two C-47s waited to fly them to Chabua.

The men did not forget their ordeal, least of all Eric Sevareid. Some months later, the journalist made a second attempt to travel to China, this time in a four-engine C-87 with Major General Harold George, chief of the ATC. Sevareid felt much safer in the four-engine plane, until shortly before landing when they hit bad weather. With visibility near zero, the pilot circled the airport at Kunming, waiting his turn to land. Fuel was low, and the men had to put on oxygen masks to breathe in the thin air at 18,000 feet. Sensing Sevareid's uneasiness, Lieutenant Colonel Rex Smith took off his mask and said to him,

"YOU DON'T DARE JUMP AGAIN, ERIC. NOBODY IN NEW YORK WOULD BELIEVE IT THIS TIME. EVEN IF THEY DID, YOUR OFFICE WOULD JUST THINK YOU HAD GOTTEN INTO A RUT AND YOUR REPUTATION WILL BE RUINED! YOU BETTER GO DOWN WITH THE PLANE!"

Fortunately that wasn't necessary. After two hours of circling, the plane landed safely, much to the newsman's great relief.

ERIC SEVAREID: JOURNALIST

Covering the events of World War II was only the start of a long and satisfying career in journalism for Eric Sevareid. He returned to the United States after the war and worked as a correspondent for CBS News in Europe, South America, Washington, and New York. In 1964 he became one of the first news analysts on prime-time television. His thoughtful editorial pieces were a staple of the CBS Evening News until his retirement in 1977.

Sevareid was also the author of six books, including *Not So Wild a Dream* (1946), an autobiography that recounted his wartime experiences in the China-Burma-India Theater. Sevareid died in 1992 at age 79.

CHAPTER 8

FLYING THE HUMP

The Hump flight from the Assam Valley in India to Kunming, China, was 500 miles and took three to four hours each way. But those could be the longest hours of an airman's life. At high altitudes, sudden winds could whip up without warning and throw a plane off course. Violent rainstorms during monsoon season and snowstorms in the winter could wreak havoc. Engines could fail, and carburetors and wings could ice up quickly in frigid temperatures.

Despite the perils, Hump crew members flew around the clock, bringing tons of precious supplies to the Chinese. Hump pilots were on 16-hour shifts and could fly up to three round-trips a day, often regardless of the weather. According to author and historian Don Moser, the only time they didn't fly was when the weather was so bad that "even the birds were grounded."

A TYPICAL FLIGHT

A pilot would typically get his flight assignment the night before and then meet his crew at the plane the next morning. Most crews were made up of a pilot, a copilot, and a radio operator. Some also had a flight engineer to monitor the instruments. On a C-46, the pilot basically ran the plane. The copilot was usually only needed to help control the plane on landing or during an emergency. The radio operator kept in communication with the airports and other planes. His role became crucial if there was trouble and the plane had to make an emergency landing at the nearest airstrip.

Before each flight the pilot and mechanic would do a quick inspection of the plane. They checked the tires and other parts to make sure everything was in working order. Between flights, mechanics would stand guard over each plane to make sure it wasn't sabotaged by natives working for the Japanese.

The cargo the planes carried included nearly everything imaginable. Weapons, ammunition, land vehicles, and fuel were the most common cargo. The planes also carried food, Chinese money, and once, even a piano. Large items, like jeeps and tanks, were sometimes taken apart to make them fit easier on the plane and then reassembled at the destination base. There was living cargo too. Horses and Chinese soldiers trained in India rode the Hump to the front lines.

In addition to items such as weapons, ammunition, and vehicles, Chinese soldiers were also transported over the Hump.

In the other direction, wounded American soldiers were headed for hospitals in India. One flight brought the bodies of dead soldiers from a Hump base to a larger burial ground in Calcutta. That time the crew had to wear oxygen masks to fend off the stench of the corpses.

Taking off from an airfield was both exhilarating and terrifying.

"I slowly pushed the throttles forward and the sudden surge of power snapped us back against the seats. The pull from the engines made us feel invincible ... Our lives were in those engines ... The runway was bumpy, the load was heavy; the plane strained to stay on the ground, bumped a little, left the runway, ... and with one sharp bump, sluggishly lifted into the night ... I could feel the weight of the load as the C-46 groaned ... Immediately, we were in the clouds—the beginning of a five-hour flight to Kunming."

—PILOT OTHA C. SPENCER DESCRIBING TAKING OFF IN HIS C-46 IN JUNE 1945

Kunming, the capital of the Chinese province of Yunnan, was the most frequent destination for Hump flights. A remote town with a mild climate, Kunming was known for its cobbled streets lined with

LOCAL LABOR

When the Hump airlift began, Dinjan was the only base in India that planes flew out of, and there was only one destination—Kunming, China. By August 1945, when the war ended with Japan, there were 13 airbases in India and six in China. All the airfields were built from scratch, mostly by native men and women. They cleared the space, leveled it, and broke rock into gravel for the surface—mostly by hand. Even the final flattening of the field was done by hand by more than 100 workers pulling huge rollers.

The airfield at Chabua became known as "the O'Hare Field of India," after the busy American airport in Chicago. Built alongside a British tea plantation, the airstrip at Chabua was lined with crumbling shacks. Other Indian airfields such as Mohanbari, Tezpur, and Warazup, were not much better.

fragrant eucalyptus trees. The Hump airlift helped turn the sleepy town into a bustling city, filled with planes coming and going at all hours of the day and night.

After landing in Kunming, local laborers known as "coolies" unloaded the cargo. Flight crews headed straight for the cafeteria. While their planes were unloaded and refueled, crew members talked or wrote letters to family and friends. If it was late at night, the crew might stay over in Kunming and leave refreshed the next morning.

BACK TO BASE

With a notably lighter plane that was easier to handle, the trip back was often less eventful. But not always. Some planes suffered engine failure or ran into bad storms on the way back. This could lead to a crash or bailout, as in the case of

Robert Crozier and his crew who found themselves stranded in Tibet.

Back at home base, pilots and crew could relax until their next assignment came through. Once they reached 650 hours of flight time, they would be rotated out and sent home. An average tour of duty flying the Hump was about seven months. Lieutenant Carl Constein was one of many crew members who kept a running record of his flight hours.

"I MADE A BIG TIME CHART AND HUNG IT ON THE WALL BETWEEN [PICTURES OF ACTRESSES] RITA HAYWORTH AND BETTY GRABLE."

"After every flight [I] rushed back to the [hut] to bring my record up to date," he wrote.

In 1945 the hours were increased to 750 and a one-year tour was required.

(The one-year tour requirement was later reduced to 10 months.) Like many men, Constein served in an office position during his additional time. "Except for two desks and chairs, the office was bare, not even a phone or a file cabinet ..." he wrote. "We'd been sent to Siberia. Report every day—and do absolutely nothing!"

Constein was among the lucky ones who ended their service in an office job. The tours of far too many airmen ended in an unmarked grave on a mountaintop or at the bottom of a jungle valley. One of the grimmest moments of a pilot's day was when he saw the day's list of dead or missing, the comrades who might never return from their last flight.

ELEPHANTS GO TO WAR

Asian elephants played an important role in the CBI Theater. These powerful and intelligent creatures are the largest land animals in the world. Because they can lift up to 600 pounds with their trunks or on their backs, they were widely used to load supplies onto Hump transport planes.

The most famous elephant handler was James "Billy" Williams, better known as "Elephant Billy." An Englishman connected with a British Special Forces unit, his company of elephants built bridges and moved supplies deep in the Burmese jungles. When Japanese troops closed in on Williams' 1,600 elephants, he led them on a incredible journey across five mountain ranges to safety in Assam, India.

CHAPTER
9

"WISHING YOU THE BEST OF LUCK"

Hump airmen had to bail out all too frequently when their planes failed.

Imagine jumping out of an airplane into unknown territory. The Hump airmen worried about the many dangers they'd encounter—rocky terrain, a steaming jungle, poisonous snakes, biting insects, and hostile tribesmen. The last thing they might expect, however, was a native who would hand them a neatly typed welcome letter. But that's exactly what the crew of a C-46 experienced when they bailed out and landed on a steep hillside in southwestern China.

The four-man crew arrived in Yankai, China, on March 29, 1944, and delivered 26 barrels of gasoline. They stayed overnight and left early the following morning for their home base in India. Robert Engels, who had piloted the plane on the trip out, switched positions with copilot Charles Allison. Rocco Commaratto, the curly-haired Italian-American crew chief, maintained and monitored all instruments and equipment on the aircraft. Edward Salay served as radio operator.

The flight went smoothly until one of the two engines began sputtering. Within moments, the engine quit. As he headed for the nearest airfield at Yunnanyi, China, 160 miles away, Allison told the crew to put on their parachutes. He silently prayed that they could make it there on one engine. But then the other engine coughed and died.

AT THAT POINT THE AIRCRAFT WAS GLIDING THROUGH THE SKY, DROPPING AT A RATE OF 1,500 FEET PER MINUTE. IT WAS TIME TO BAIL OUT—FAST.

Allison joined the others at the rear cargo door. They had already opened the small hatch but were arguing over who should jump first. Allison made the decision for them and jumped. The others quickly followed.

A STRANGE WELCOME

On the way down the airmen passed through a snowstorm and shivered from the cold. They were almost on the ground when they heard their plane crash. Three of them landed safely on a 3,000-foot hillside above the Salween River. Commaratto landed in a tree and was immediately helped down by some Lisu tribesmen who lived nearby.

After the crew members were reunited, they descended the hill to the valley below. Minutes later, a smiling tribesman handed Allison a letter. What he read was astonishing.

From the Tibetan-Lisuland Churches of Christ

December 15, 1943

To All Grounded USA Fliers: Dear Sirs:
It is indeed unfortunate that you have been grounded in this Valley, but the USAAF [U.S. Army Air Forces], in lookout for just such an eventuality, has enlisted our assistance in preparing for you, in this Valley. So don't lose courage.

The letter went on to say that the Lisu people would guide them to the mission in Latsa in China's Yunnan province. The missionaries had even provided paper and an envelope so the airmen could write down their names, medical needs, and who should be notified of their situation. A native runner would bring the note to the mission. The letter ended:

Wishing you the best of luck, and Godspeed on your journey back to civilization, we remain,

Sincerely,

Eugene R. Morse

The men immediately resolved to get to the mission. But before they left the Lisu village, they went to see what was left of their downed plane. In heavy rains they crossed the Salween River on a raft and found an awful sight. Even in the downpour, the plane was still burning. Soon there would be nothing left of it but a blackened shell.

Accompanied by Lisu guides and carriers, the four men followed the river to the village of Lissadi. The following day, while eating a dinner prepared by the villagers, they saw a small white man enter with an escort of Lisu tribesmen. He introduced himself as Robert Morse, the 24-year-old son of the mission's head, Russell Morse. He said he had heard of their arrival through the natives' drumming, which he called "jungle telegraph."

Morse explained that the Air Force had asked for their help in finding downed American pilots in the region. They had distributed welcome letters to Lisu natives in the area, many of whom the missionaries had converted to Christianity. They told the Lisu to be on the lookout for lost airmen.

TO THE MISSION

Morse offered to guide the Americans to the mission himself. They left the next day. The Lisu scrambled up the mountain trails with ease, even while carrying their long, razor-sharp knives and crossbows with poison-tipped arrows. But for the Americans it was a grueling trek, so difficult that they had to rest every half hour.

To avoid the worst climbing, Morse led them on the "Monkey Trail," a narrow path that clung to the sides of cliffs, about 1,000 feet above the Salween River. The Americans trembled with each step. As they crossed a rickety bamboo bridge over an opening in the trail, Engels slipped. To break his fall, he grabbed onto a thick bush. But he could feel the plant's roots being yanked out of the ground.

**HE WAS ONLY SECONDS AWAY
FROM PLUNGING TO HIS DEATH FAR BELOW
WHEN COMMARATTO RUSHED DOWN AND
PULLED HIM UP TO SAFETY.**

They left the "Monkey Trail" with a sigh of relief, but the next leg of the journey wasn't any easier. In a drenching downpour, they climbed a steep, 2,000-foot slope. Then, through the pelting rains, they saw it—the mission at Latsa. For the weary, rain-soaked Americans, it was like entering the Land of Oz. Robert's brother Eugene and their father, Russell, were both away when the airmen arrived. But they received a warm greeting from Robert's mother, Helen, and her adopted Tibetan daughters. The airmen settled in for the night, using their parachutes for bedding.

The rain continued without letting up the next morning. Russell and Eugene Morse arrived the next day. Russell, who had spent much of his adult life in this remote region of Asia, told them it would take a month to reach Fort Hertz, the American base in northern Burma.

Hoping that a search plane would spot them, the airmen sent out signals from a hilltop. But the nearly constant rain made visibility poor, so planes flew by without seeing them. Finally on April 18, a B-25 bomber circled overhead—it was a sure sign that they had been spotted. The next day a rescue plane dropped packages of food and a walkie-talkie, so the men could communicate with the plane's pilot.

As much as they were pleased with the supply drops, the men wished the plane— any plane—would come down and take them home. But there was no place in this remote, mountainous region for even the smallest of aircraft to land. They had no option but to walk out. And so on April 29, the four airmen, Eugene and Russell Morse, and 30 native bearers, headed for Fort Hertz. It would be the adventure of a lifetime.

A FAMILY OF MISSIONARIES

The Morse mission in Asia started long before the outbreak of World War II and endured long after it ended. J. Russell and Gertrude Morse first came to China in 1921 to work under the missionary Dr. Albert Shelton. Only months after their arrival, Dr. Shelton was attacked by Tibetan bandits and died in Morse's arms. Four years later the couple began their own mission in Yunnan province.

After World War II, the mission faced new challenges. When the Communists took over China in 1949, J. Russell was jailed for his Christian beliefs and spent 15 months in solitary confinement. The family and their mission workers fled to northern Burma where they thrived for 15 years. But in 1966 a military dictatorship came to power in Burma, and they were forced to leave.

Since 1973 the Morse mission has been based in Thailand. It is currently run by Joni Morse, the grandson of J. Russell, who died in 1991.

DANGERS
GALORE

Bad weather, faulty aircraft, and treacherous mountains posed the greatest dangers for the Hump airmen. But these weren't the only challenges they faced. There were other perils lurking that could be just as deadly.

ENEMIES IN THE AIR

The difficult route over the Himalayas was chosen in part because it discouraged the enemy from flying there. Even so, Hump pilots did encounter the enemy from time to time.

"I would rather fly ... against the [Japanese] three times a day than fly a transport over the [H]ump once."

—LIEUTENANT TOMMY HARMON, FIGHTER PILOT

The heavy transport planes were ill-equipped to defend themselves if they ran into fighter planes, such as Japanese Zeroes or Bettys. The pilots' only weapons were pistols and machine guns, which weren't much help thousands of feet in the air. In most cases, the pilots had to rely on their flying skills to escape the firepower of the attacking Japanese planes.

An attack could come as suddenly as a wind gust or storm. One C-46 crew was on its way to Kunming with a load of ammunition when several Japanese Zeroes suddenly surrounded their plane. The Zeroes' gunfire struck the C-46's left engine and cargo bay.

"SUDDENLY A BURST CAME UP THROUGH THE COCKPIT FLOOR," RECALLED COPILOT GEORGE J. PLAVA. "WE SAW DAYLIGHT THROUGH THE HOLE."

Oil pressure in the damaged engine dropped, and the plane rapidly fell 2,000 feet. With the aircraft coming dangerously

a Japanese Zero fighter plane

close to the mountaintops, pilot Tom Withers gave the order to bail out, and the entire crew parachuted into a valley in northern Burma. Fortunately for them, they were greeted by friendly Kachin tribesmen who helped them navigate the jungle and find Fort Hertz.

CAUGHT BY SURPRISE

Sometimes Hump airmen were simply unlucky enough to be in the wrong place at the wrong time. In mid-January 1945, pilot Joseph Plosser was taking off when he saw several flashing red and green lights coming toward his C-87. He realized with a shock that it was five Japanese Bettys. With a clearance of less than 50 feet on either wing, Plosser flew between the enemy planes and soared upward to escape them just in time. The Bettys dropped bombs on the runway, blowing up two American aircraft.

At times the airmen deliberately flew into harm's way. On February 15, 1945, a C-47 flew into Japanese-occupied Burma to deliver several bags of mule feed to American forces fighting there. As he approached the drop-off site, pilot

Ryan Dawdy descended to 500 feet to drop his cargo. Suddenly Japanese guns on the ground opened fire, puncturing the plane's right side and tail. If they bailed out, Dawdy and his crew would certainly be captured by the Japanese. Instead, Dawdy ordered the crew to dump the cargo at once and then race to the rear of the plane. The shift of weight helped the plane climb into the sky. At 3,000 feet, Dawdy told the men to move to the center of the aircraft, which allowed him to level the plane and stabilize it. He then set his course for the British base at Bhama, Burma, where he landed safely.

NATURE'S KAMIKAZES

There were other high fliers—nonhuman ones—that posed unexpected dangers for the airmen. Birds nesting on the sides of cliffs or mountains could attack a plane with just as much determination as any Japanese pilot. A bird's mangled body in a plane's engine could do serious damage and even bring down an aircraft.

"They [the birds] seemed to have a kamikaze death-wish that [ensured] them a special [place] in bird [heaven] if they died attacking a DC-3, B-25, or B-24."

—Hump historian Milton Miller

As part of a celebration of Air Force Day on August 1, 1945, a group of B-25s in Barrackpore, India, was disrupted by a seagull. The bird hit the edge of one plane's wing, breaking the oil and fuel lines. Fortunately, the pilot was able to land the plane safely, but it took three weeks to repair the damaged aircraft.

Other times encounters with birds were more a discomfort than a serious danger.

One time a Hump chaplain, who was disliked by the men, was heading home to the United States. During the flight, a large bird crashed through the glass window near where the chaplain was seated. A crewman found the unfortunate pastor covered in the dead bird's blood, feathers, and body parts. When the plane landed in India, the terrible experience appeared to have transformed the wayward chaplain. "He was convinced that he had received a special message," claimed one airman who saw him. "He now preached love and his voice was loud, clear and sincere."

GERM WARFARE

Disease was a less visible but no less serious danger for the men on the ground and in the air. Malaria was common throughout the military bases in India and in the jungles of Burma. This disease comes from mosquito bites and causes high fever, chills, and sometimes death. Every day, all crew members and personnel were required to take a pill to prevent them from getting malaria. The medicine turned the person's skin yellow, making it easy to spot a newcomer to the Hump by his normal skin tone.

There were other illnesses just as widespread in the region. "Dhobie itch" was a rash that tormented some airmen for their entire tour on the Hump. Even more troublesome was dysentery, a disease that attacked the digestive system and led to chronic diarrhea and dehydration.

Lack of oxygen at high altitudes could bring about a serious condition called anoxemia, which causes a lack of oxygen in the blood. Airmen who parachuted onto mountaintops often experienced this condition until they descended to lower, oxygen-richer altitudes. But if an aircraft experienced an oxygen leak, anoxemia could strike on board a plane as well. Pilot Bill Spatz unknowingly suffered anoxemia inside his plane when his oxygen mask failed to work. After being discharged from the service, Spatz developed a mysterious ailment related to anoxemia. He died years later from the illness.

THE ENEMY WITHIN

Perhaps the most surprising and ironic peril faced by the Hump airmen came from within their own ranks. The anxiety of flying the Hump took its toll—both physically and mentally—on pilots and crew. Some couldn't take the pressure and turned "Hump happy." They took reckless risks on flights that endangered the whole crew. Doctors regularly examined Hump pilots for signs of a mental breakdown. If necessary, pilots were sent immediately to Calcutta or another city to rest.

Some pilots simply froze in panic in the heat of the moment. Copilot Carl Constein recalled a near-fatal flight with a pilot. When an engine failed and the plane began to fall from the sky, the pilot froze with fear. Constein took control and guided the plane to the airfield. At the last second, the pilot regained control and landed the plane safely at Yunnanyi, China. Once they were on the ground, the pilot tried to make excuses for his meltdown. But as Constein later recalled,

"I KNEW THIS: I WOULD REFUSE TO FLY WITH HIM AGAIN."

A NEVER-ENDING
NIGHTMARE

After bailing out of their plane in southwestern China, Allison, Engels, Commaratto, and Salay were treated kindly by the Morse family of American missionaries. But the only way back to Fort Hertz in Burma was to walk there. From the start it was a difficult trek for the American airmen and Eugene and Russell Morse. But their Lisu bearers scrambled up and down the steep, rocky trails as sure-footed as mountain goats. And they were lugging up to 75 pounds of supplies on their backs!

The group soon reached the Salween River on the first leg of their journey to Fort Hertz. To cross, each person sat on a seat attached to strong ropes equipped with rollers that spanned the river. They were pushed off from one side, propelled across the river, and arrived on the other side at a lower point from where they started.

Similar to modern-day zip lines, ropes and rollers were used by natives to cross swift-flowing rivers.

A TREACHEROUS JOURNEY

The trails they were treading were dangerously slick with mud from the persistent rains. One of the Lisu tribesmen even slipped and went tumbling down a mountainside. When Eugene Morse went to his aid, he also slid down the slippery slope. The two men fell 400 feet before coming to a stop.

Soon after that incident, the Lisu carriers announced that they were returning home. Only Russell Morse's promise of an extra day's pay persuaded them to continue.

The group tried to cross the mountains at a pass, but driving rain and bitter cold drove them back. They tried again at another spot, and this time reached the top of the pass at an elevation of 12,000 feet. They were now near the border of western

China and eastern Burma. As they made their descent, the ground was so slick with mud that they were able to slide down part of the way. They used wooden sticks to steer their bodies like oars on a boat.

As they came down from the mountains, they returned to the hot, sweaty jungle terrain. Their feet sank into mud that was a foot deep in some places. Here they stumbled upon the skeletons of Chinese soldiers who had died when the Japanese overtook Burma two years earlier. It was a chilling reminder of the war they had almost forgotten was still raging around them.

BLOOD-SUCKING LEECHES AND GIANT KILLER BEES

More and more the march to Fort Hertz was becoming a never-ending nightmare. Allison had a serious case of poison ivy.

Eugene Morse had blisters on his feet and found it difficult to walk. His father was suffering from a sinus infection. And everyone was plagued by leeches.

THEY WOULD SINK THEIR JAWS INTO ARMS, LEGS, AND TORSOS AND FEED ON THE VICTIMS' BLOOD.

If a victim managed to tear off the leech's body, the jaws often remained embedded in the skin. The nearly naked native carriers could spot the leeches immediately on their bodies and expertly flicked them off cleanly with a stick. The Americans often wouldn't find them until they removed their clothes at night. Then they had to get the leeches off as quickly as possible to avoid serious infection. In a letter to his father, Engels reported that he once scraped 21 leeches off his legs.

LEECHES

There are hundreds of species of leeches, but only a few of them suck the blood of animals and humans for food. A few kinds of leeches live on moist land in tropical jungles,

but most thrive in water, such as streams, rivers, lakes, and even oceans. When a victim comes near, the blood-sucking leeches are drawn by its scent and latch onto the skin with suckers that have sharp, tiny teeth. A chemical in their saliva prevents the blood from thickening and keeps it flowing freely.

But leeches were not always seen as the enemy. For centuries, doctors used leeches to "bleed" their patients. The bleeding was thought to help people recover from various illnesses. Leeches are still used in traditional Chinese and Indian medicine. Although they are rarely used in Western medicine today, they are sometimes used to treat people who are allergic to prescription blood-thinning medicines.

There were deadly insects to contend with as well. Enormous bees, measuring an inch and a half long, buzzed around their heads. "We passed two graves of Englishmen who had been stung by these bees," Engels wrote to his father.

"ONE STING IN THE THROAT PROVED FATAL TO ONE AND A STING ON THE HEAD TO THE OTHER.

We wore headnets sometimes, but the heat made them unbearable at times."

The hikers lived on a diet that included rice, eggs, and some chicken. They supplemented this meager fare with edible plants they found including fern leaves, bamboo shoots, and cinnamon bark. Desperately hungry, the airmen bought food at one village only to find that it was covered with mold and was inedible.

At another village they slept in a shack infested with fleas and lice that bit them mercilessly all night.

THE NIGHTMARE ENDS

After spending a night in the village of Redum, Allison, Engels, and Commaratto decided to push on for Konglu. Salay and the Morses stayed behind to rest. Allison, Engels, and Commaratto reached Konglu late in the afternoon on June 20. The three airmen were welcomed warmly by the American soldiers stationed in the remote outpost. They were given food, and for the first time on their long journey slept peacefully in hammocks. The missionaries and Salay arrived the following afternoon.

The food supply at Konglu was running low, so Allison—the healthiest of the bunch—headed to Fort Hertz the next day. He hoped to find help and food along the way and have it sent back to the others in Konglu. He arrived at Fort Hertz about a month later accompanied by a sergeant and native bearers.

Not content with waiting around to be rescued, the others left a few days after Allison. They arrived at Fort Hertz three days after him. There they rested, ate, and for the first time since leaving Latsa were treated with medical supplies. After a week of bad weather, a C-47 landed on the small airfield. Allison flew back to their home base in India, leaving the others behind to recuperate. He arrived at Chabua 93 days after leaving. The others arrived soon after. Their long nightmare was over. In a letter to his father dated July 1, Engels wrote:

"IT WAS QUITE AN EXPERIENCE, BUT I WOULDN'T WANT TO GO THROUGH IT AGAIN."

The airmen didn't forget the debt they owed to the Morse family. They sent the missionaries' requests for supplies to the Air Force. Soon the mission received all the food and goods it needed to keep operating.

CHAPTER
12

BIG CHANGES ON
THE HUMP

General William H. Tunner

Things had basically stayed the same at the base in Chabua while Allison and his crew were gone. But that was about to change. In August 1944 General William H. Tunner took over command of Hump operations from General Tom Hardin. Tunner was a disciplinarian whose toughness had earned him the nickname "Willie the Whip."

He was determined to make the Hump flights even more efficient and productive than they had been under Hardin. But to do so, he realized that he had to improve the men's morale. Hammie Heard, one of his aides, reported that morale was at an all-time low. "This is grim," he said. "Everyone wants to go home—getting out of here is all they think about."

IMPROVING MORALE

To change this situation Tunner set out to make life on base more restful and pleasant. He ordered trucks with food and drinks onto the flight line where planes were loaded, unloaded, and serviced. He established 24-hour cafeterias so airmen could eat at any time, day or night. He also encouraged airmen to take short vacations between flights to China or India.

And he ordered daily full-dress inspections to see that the men took more pride in their appearance.

Just as importantly, Tunner disregarded Hardin's rule that the men would fly regardless of weather conditions on the Hump. Instead pilots were told that if the weather was very bad, they could turn their planes around and come back to base to wait until conditions were better. Safety programs for crews were also put into place. Due to these efforts, the general achieved what some thought impossible—increased flights and tonnage and at the same time fewer accidents.

August 22 was declared "Tom Hardin Day," in honor of the ATC's former commander. The goal was to set a record for the number of Hump flights in 24 hours.

By the end of the day, 308 flights were made and 1,300 tons of supplies had flown into China. That was more tonnage than was delivered during the entire first month of the Hump's operation.

SEARCH AND RESCUE

Tunner also improved search-and-rescue (SAR) missions along the Hump route. Such missions had been underway since August 1943, but they used fewer men and a handful of older planes. It proved to be a less-than-effective operation in finding lost airmen in the hills, mountains, and jungles along the Hump route. But General Tunner got approval from Washington to enlarge the operation and improve its efficiency. He centered it in Mohanbari, India, with a team of 12 officers and 44 enlisted men with newer, better aircraft. Within a month, the number of men on the SAR team had doubled. By war's end, the SAR squadron had saved 1,171 of the 2,830 crewmen who had gone down over the Hump. There were still 345 missing, and 1,314 had been confirmed dead.

In the steamy jungles of Burma, the new SAR squadron was about to prove its effectiveness in the daring rescue of a downed pilot whose situation seemed hopeless. The soldier who risked his own life to bring the pilot back would become one of the Hump's most colorful and celebrated heroes.

THE LEDO ROAD

While the Hump air route continued to be the main source of supplies, a new land route opened from India to China in early 1945. Army engineers and thousands of American soldiers and Indian laborers under the direction of General Lewis Pick built the road. It began in Ledo, India, and passed over the Naga Hills and the Patkai mountains. From there, it crossed northern Burma where it met up with the Burma Road, which ended in China. A pipeline was laid along this new road to provide fuel to American troops in China. Nonmilitary goods and items too big to fit inside a Hump airplane, such as heavy equipment and large trucks, could be driven along the road. The new road was initially called Pick's Pike, but it was later renamed the Ledo Road.

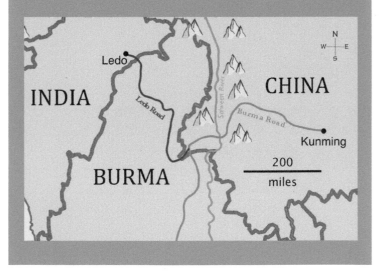

13

ALONE IN THE JUNGLE

Not every aircraft that went down on the Hump route was a transport plane. Fighter planes sometimes had to cross the Hump to get from one location to the next. They often failed and crashed too. Fighter pilots and their crews who were lucky enough to bail out in time were also the object of search-and-rescue missions. On July 29, 1944, Second Lieutenant Greenlaw Collins joined their number when his P-51 fighter plane went down.

STRANDED IN THE JUNGLE

When Collins, who was flying solo, lost control of his plane, he knew he had to get out—and fast. He flung open the hatch and parachuted out. Down, down, down he fell through the sky like a lead weight. When the parachute popped open, he gasped with relief. He floated through the thick, humid air, landing with a bump in a tree on a mountain slope near the Gedu River in northern Burma. He managed to swing himself down to a branch in another tree. But when he did, the branch that his parachute was caught on broke. To save himself from tumbling down the mountain with the tree branch and the chute, Collins unbuckled his harness and slid to the ground.

Collins was lucky to reach the ground safely and uninjured, but he was unlucky too. His emergency pack, which contained useful tools and food for survival, was attached to the harness high up in the tree, out of reach. All he had was a cup, a canteen, a fountain pen, a wallet, a cigarette lighter that was out of fluid, and four matches. That wasn't much help for someone stranded in the jungle.

But then the downed pilot heard the distinct hum of an airplane. He looked up and saw what he thought to be a search-and-rescue plane circling overhead. He raced down the mountainside to the river and started a small fire with the matches. Hoping to signal the plane, Collins waved his shirt wildly in the air.

BUT THE PLANE FLEW AWAY.
THE PILOT HADN'T SEEN HIM.

Discouraged, Collins waited for nightfall and found a flat rock to sleep on. The next morning he decided to stay where he was, convinced that he would soon be spotted by a rescue pilot. He figured that by then, his comrades back at base would realize he was missing. Although he saw several planes go by just 500 feet or less overhead, they didn't appear to see him and flew off.

Another day passed. Then a third. On the sixth day, Collins decided that he had to start moving and find help. If he didn't, he knew he wouldn't survive for long.

He followed the Gedu River as much as possible, detouring around mountains when ravines broke up the route. Some of the slopes were so steep and thick with underbrush that at times he had to crawl on his belly like a snake. His leather boots were falling apart, his feet were covered with painful blisters, and leeches had left bleeding wounds on his arms and legs. He ate whatever berries and fruits he could find, as well as locusts and even butterflies. At night, he covered himself with leaves and grass to keep his body warm in the freezing temperatures.

LIVING AMONG THE NAGA

Eleven days into his ordeal, Collins found a hut on an island in the river. He went inside, laid down, and slept, sheltered from the rain and wind. On his fourth day in the hut, he saw figures approaching. They were members of the Naga tribe. And to Collins' great relief, they greeted him as a friend.

The Naga fed him, and despite not sharing a common language, they were able to communicate through hand gestures and facial expressions. Realizing that Collins was in no shape to travel, the tribesmen stayed with him in the hut for four days before taking him to their village. Even with the extended rest, Collins was too weak to walk very far, so the Naga built a litter and carried him the rest of the way. As they entered the small village, a village elder took charge of the unexpected guest. He took the pilot to his hut and fed him cooked monkey meat and rice.

COLLINS HAD HIGH HOPES THAT A RESCUE PLANE WOULD COME LOOKING FOR HIM, BUT DAYS PASSED WITH NO PLANE IN SIGHT.

Although the natives were thoughtful and caring, they had no medicine to ease his pain or improve his health. Collins was suffering from malnutrition and infected blisters on his legs and feet. He was unable to walk so he stayed in the hut. He lay on a bamboo mat with a log for a pillow, staring into the small fire that kept him warm at night. He feared he would die there, alone and forgotten by the outside world, buried by the Naga in an unmarked grave.

A DESPERATE NOTE

Then one day a group of Naga tribesmen arrived in the village. Although they could only communicate with gestures, Collins believed they had been sent by the army as a search party. Grabbing a pencil, he summoned the strength to scrawl a note on a scrap of paper.

"I am the pilot who crashed and am coming in with Nagas, but to make it I need shoes, medical supplies, including quinine, and a blanket. "I am ashamed, asking for so much..

Lieutenant G.M. Collins"

The search-party members agreed to take the note to the nearest American outpost. It was Collins' last hope.

Time passed. With each day, Collins lost a little more hope, and his health continued to decline. With his legs and feet covered with blisters, he couldn't even make it as far as the edge of the village. He lay there in the hut half awake, half asleep.

One day a darkened figure entered his hut. The man stood looking down at him just a few feet away. Collins' eyes welled up with tears. The stranger dropped to his knees and grasped the pilot's trembling hand. It was an American soldier. Collins managed to weakly murmur:

"THANK THE ALMIGHTY. YOU'VE COME."

His ordeal was far from over, but he was no longer alone.

DIEBOLD TO THE RESCUE

William Diebold stood listening with some interest to the conversation between several pilots and Major Roland Hedrick, his new commanding officer. They were having a heated discussion about Lieutenant Greenlaw Collins, a downed pilot stranded in the Gedu River Valley. Collins' desperate note had arrived at the base a day or so earlier.

Hedrick explained that a rescue plane had been sent out to find the village where Collins was staying. Two army doctors were ready to parachute into the village and care for Collins until he was well enough to be brought out by land. But the search-and-rescue pilot found two villages on two mountaintops and didn't know which one was the right village. He dropped notes in packs on the villages, but there was no signal from either village indicating where Collins was. That meant he wasn't in either village or was too weak to come out and give the plane a signal.

Diebold listened and then suggested that maybe one man could parachute into one village and, if the pilot wasn't there, investigate the other. Once he located Collins, the doctors could then be dropped down. The major thought it was a good idea. But they'd have to find a volunteer for this risky mission, and the base was already shorthanded.

A RELUCTANT VOLUNTEER

"Major, I'll jump," said Diebold. The words were no sooner out of his mouth than the soldier had second thoughts. He was brand new to the 1352nd Search and Rescue Squadron and was only assigned to it temporarily. More importantly, he had never jumped out of an airplane before.

But before Diebold could change his mind, the major accepted his offer. He sent Diebold to be outfitted for the jungle, and told him to report back within the hour. Before he knew it, Diebold was nervously standing in a C-47, flying over the mountains of northern Burma. He was armed with a pistol, ammunition, and a bag of silver rupees, the Indian currency. The pistol was for poisonous snakes or other unfriendly creatures. The rupees were for the Naga natives, who would be more willing to assist him if they were paid for their help.

The plane's pilot, a friendly Texan named Johnny "Andy" Anderson, was astonished to hear that his passenger had never used a parachute before. He gave Diebold some quick tips and then told him to wait at the plane's rear door for a bell, his signal to jump.

"The bell rang, and the next thing I knew was the roaring of the slip-stream in my ears, the tumbling of the horizon, the tail of the ship passing overhead ... and then the almighty jerk [as the parachute opened]."

—Lieutenant William Diebold recalling the first time he jumped from an airplane

As Diebold floated down, his terror turned to relief and then joy. But as the ground rushed up at him, the fear returned, clutching at his throat. Diebold landed on a tree stump but with all his bones intact. No sooner had he gotten to his feet than villagers appeared, saying, "O.K.—O.K.," over and over, reassuring him of their good intentions with the only English word they seemed to know.

AMONG THE HEADHUNTERS

Diebold heard the plane passing overhead and looked up to see more parachutes descending from the sky. Diebold and the villagers had to dodge being hit by these packages of supplies. Once on the ground, the Naga quickly retrieved the packs. One contained a radio and a walkie-talkie that Diebold could use to communicate with the pilot. Another held an emergency medical kit. The villagers were able to communicate with their hands that Collins was not in their village. However, they assured him that they knew where Collins was and would take him there the following day.

The village elder led Diebold into a hut where a disturbing collection of dried shrunken heads was on display. He had heard that the Naga were headhunters.

Diebold later wrote with grim humor:

"I BEGAN TO PICK THE SPOT WHERE THEY'D PROBABLY PUT MINE."

Later he learned that the heads on the wall were from animals not people.

The next morning they left for the village of Geda Ga. The jungle was nearly impenetrable, with fields of grass 10 feet tall and a solid wall of vines, bushes, and trees. Then there were the leeches. Diebold could see them all over his body, sucking his blood. When they reached a river, he and the Naga waded into the cold water. His helpful guides skillfully picked the leeches off his skin.

"They were all over me. I tried to flick a few ... off, but they'd catch onto my fingers and hang on. It was like trying to throw away chewing gum."

—LIEUTENANT WILLIAM DIEBOLD FROM HIS BOOK *HELL IS SO GREEN*

Later that afternoon they arrived at the other mountaintop. There stood a tiny village composed of just two huts. At one hut an old man with wrinkled skin invited him to come inside. In the first room, Diebold saw a man lying on the floor, his head turned away toward a small fire. It was Collins, and he was in terrible shape. He was extremely weak, thin as a rail, and had a long, scraggly beard. After they shook hands, Diebold assured the pilot that two doctors were on their way to help him.

Diebold opened his kit and cooked up some hot cereal and tea on the fire. The weakened Collins ate and drank only a little before falling asleep. Diebold went outside and saw the C-47 circling above. Two more parachutes blossomed in the blue sky. It was the doctors, Major Bill Spruell and Captain

Sandy Morrissey. One landed in the village and the other in the jungle where the Naga quickly retrieved him. They were both as calm and collected as if they had just popped by for a house call.

The doctors immediately checked on their patient. They treated Collins' leg with a healing ointment and gave him blood plasma to replace lost blood and help his body fight infection. They also cut his long hair and dressed him in clean clothes.

A RISKY PROPOSITION

The doctors said Collins would make a full recovery, but only if they could get him out of the jungle and back to civilization quickly. If he remained where he was in his present condition, the doctors felt his chances of survival were slim.

The question was *how* were they going to get him out? Even given some time to recuperate, Collins would be in no condition to walk out on his own. They could try to carry him out on a litter. But they would have to widen the narrow jungle path for miles and miles—an impossible task. Diebold came up with a third option. They could put Collins on a litter, tie him to a raft, and float him down the Gedu River to civilization and help. The doctors were a bit skeptical, but they were willing to give it a try. But when Diebold radioed the plan to pilot Anderson, he was dead-set against it. Anderson had followed the river's violent twists and turns from the air and thought it was too dangerous. But Diebold persisted, and the pilot finally agreed to drop them an inflatable raft.

While they waited for Collins to recuperate for the journey, the Naga made a litter out of bamboo. But before they could start down the river, they first had to get Collins down the mountain, a difficult feat in itself. Two Naga men led the way, slashing the thick vegetation to make a path wide enough for the litter and the men carrying it.

They arrived at the river in late afternoon and camped for the night. The Naga men caught a deer and a monkey and served them for dinner. That night, the three rescuers made plans for the morning. The section of the river they were at was filled with nasty bends and swift rapids. They could try to carry the raft and Collins further downriver, where it was smoother sailing. But they would have to get past some sheer rock walls that could prove just as treacherous. Instead they decided to use the parachutes' cords to make a rope. They would then tie one end to the raft and wrap the other end around a boulder. One of them would let out the line from the boulder end and slowly guide the raft down the rapids.

RUNNING THE RAPIDS

In the morning they all put on life jackets that had been dropped from the plane. Then Morrissey got into the raft with Collins. Spruell waited at the first curve to help push the raft around the rocks. Diebold looped the rope line around a boulder and waited. Morrissey gave the raft a shove into the water and jumped on board. The rapids tossed the raft around like a paper plate. Diebold held on to the line for dear life, but a moment later, it snapped.

THE BOAT SHOT FORWARD DOWN THE RAPIDS LIKE AN ARROW AND RAMMED INTO THE ROCK WALL.

It spun backward and then continued down to the next bend where it once again slammed into the rocks.

As Spruell tried to push the raft off the wall, he tumbled into the rapids. Diebold lost sight of him in the churning waters. While running down the riverbank to catch up to the raft, Diebold promptly slipped and fell in too. As the waters swept Diebold along, he hit his head on a rock wall and was knocked unconscious. When he came to, he was rushing downriver. If he hadn't been wearing a life jacket, he would have surely drowned. Diebold spotted the raft beached on a sandbar with the two doctors busy bailing out the water inside.

After a brief rest, they tried again. This time everyone got into the raft with Collins secured on the bottom in the litter. "Good heavens," he muttered, raising his head to look over the side at the rocks and rapids ahead.

"I'D RATHER BAIL OUT OVER THE HUMP ANYTIME THAN TAKE ANOTHER TRIP LIKE THIS ONE."

They floated into a monstrous whirlpool and spun around and around, until they eventually bounced off some rocks. They were just getting their breath back when Morrissey spotted a waterfall ahead. The waterfall was only 2 feet high, but the rubber raft flew into the air then slammed into the river bottom. The raft immediately began to fill with water and sink. "Grab that limb!" Morrissey cried as they floated under a dangling tree branch. Diebold clutched the limb and held on as the raft turned around swiftly and came to rest on the riverbank.

The men were soaked to the bone and shivering with cold, but they were alive. Morrissey and Diebold built a fire and made coffee. As they were warming up, a plane came into sight. Those in the plane saw the fire and the yellow raft and circled back around. A crew member at the rear door of the plane flashed signal lights to communicate some good news. About 5 miles downriver at the junction with the larger Tarung River, motorboats sent by Major Hedrick were waiting for them.

The rest of the ride was as bumpy and wild as a roller coaster. But the men took it in stride, knowing that the end of their ordeal was near. When they reached the river junction, they saw three large barges with motors. They lifted Collins and the rubber raft onto one of the barges. All day they rode in style in the larger boats, safe from the twists and turns of the river. During the night, they arrived at the Ledo Road where an ambulance was waiting. After they loaded Collins in, he shook Diebold's hand and told him,

"THANKS IS A SMALL WORD TO USE WHEN YOU'VE SAVED MY LIFE ..."

But it was the only word that Lieutenant Diebold needed to hear.

The next day, the trio of rescuers were picked up by a search-and-rescue plane that carried them back to Assam. Diebold had thrived on the excitement and danger of the mission. He also felt good about saving

Soldiers carried a very weak Lieutenant Collins to a barge. He'd lost 55 pounds, but his long ordeal was almost over.

a fellow soldier who without him probably would have died. He decided that maybe his assignment to SAR wouldn't be so temporary after all.

CHAPTER 15

SAVING SERGEANT
BIG FOOT

Marvin Jacobs' decision to take a nap on board the C–46 carrying him back to Karachi, India, saved his life. Of the more than 27 people aboard the plane on February 3, 1945, the Hump radio operator was the only one to survive its crash. Jacobs had gone back to the rear of the plane and was lying on a pile of bags when the plane went down.

SOLE SURVIVOR

The next thing Jacobs knew, he was stuck in a thicket of bamboo in heavy rain. He was bleeding, and his leg was throbbing. Local natives found him and gave him food and shelter for the night. The next morning he visited the charred remains of his plane. It was a grim moment, especially when he found two of his close friends among the dead.

The natives built a bamboo litter and carried the injured airman to their village. The villagers fed him potatoes and popcorn, but they had no medicine to help heal his aching foot, which grew more swollen by the day. Desperate for help, Jacobs wrote a note explaining his location and predicament. He gave it to a native runner who carried it to a nearby British tea plantation. The plantation manager sent supplies of food and drink back to the village. He also passed the information about the downed airman on to the American Search and Rescue Squadron.

Major Hedrick turned the case over to Lieutenant Diebold, who had recently rescued Greenlaw Collins. Diebold had a partner now, Sergeant James Brenner, a hardened, gray-haired veteran. For all their differences, the two men shared a love for action and adventure and both had a good sense of humor. Together they made a winning team.

Diebold and Brenner parachuted into the jungle near a village where they hoped Jacobs was holed up. A village elder had no information on his whereabouts and sent them to a second village. The chief of this other village told them an American with "a big foot" was staying in a village to the north. Diebold decided this was most likely Jacobs, the man they were searching for.

The following day they set off with six native bearers. When they reached the village, Diebold was led to a hut. There, lying on the floor was a skeleton of a man, with a scraggly beard and a foot swollen to twice its normal size. The first words from the injured man's mouth stunned his rescuer. He offered Diebold a drink saying, "You look like you need one." Brenner and Diebold were hopeful that Jacobs would make it back alive, although it looked likely that his injured foot would have to be amputated.

Diebold radioed Bill Davis, the rescue plane pilot, and told him to drop off the doctor on board, Austin Lamberts. Dr. Lamberts made a grand entrance, landing with his chute tangled in a large tree in the center of the village. Uninjured, he immediately checked on his patient. The news was surprisingly good. Jacobs' foot would not need to be amputated, but it would be several months before he could walk on it. Diebold knew they couldn't wait that long, and to try to carry Jacobs out in a litter was impractical given the narrow trails and rough terrain.

AN AIRFIELD IN THE WILDERNESS

Diebold saw only one option—fly Jacobs out in a plane. However, for a plane to land they needed an airfield, and there was none. Diebold proposed making a landing strip, one just big enough for a light plane to land and take off. Brenner and Lamberts were intrigued by the idea. However, they pointed out that they had seen no place in the area that was flat enough to make even a small airstrip.

Diebold got on his walkie-talkie and asked Davis to fly around and see if he could find a spot for a makeshift airstrip. The pilot found a flat area in a valley a few miles from the village, so Diebold went to check it out. Brenner, meanwhile, was sent on a grimmer mission. Accompanied by some natives, he went to the wreckage site of the C-46 to bury the dead. He also retrieved three mailbags and any personal effects that could be given to loved ones.

Diebold felt the field was about the right size. But it was dotted with hundreds of tree stumps left by the natives when they turned it into a cornfield. Tall grass and dead cornstalks had to be cut down. The trees that lined either end of the field also had to be cut back to allow more room for the plane to take off.

Clearing the field would be a monumental job, but Diebold felt they had no choice but to give it a try. He knew they could count on the natives for manpower as long as they were paid for their labor. He got on the walkie-talkie and told Davis he'd need 12 pickaxes, 12 axes, 12 shovels, six cross-cut saws, 200 rupees, and five cases of dynamite. They would need the dynamite to blow up the larger stumps.

They spread the word that the Americans were hiring workers to clear the field. Soon more than 200 men, women, and children showed up eager to get to work. Diebold set the tall grass and nearby woods on fire to get started. To everyone's surprise, this set off a stampede of wild animals, including rabbits, deer, and wild boars. Diebold grabbed his gun and started shooting. The natives joined in the hunt with their bows and arrows. Together, they brought down more than 100 animals. Everyone ate fresh meat that night.

The next day, everybody went to work. The women cut grass, the children carried it away, and the men hauled off fallen timber. However, Diebold quickly grew frustrated with his workers, who were not accustomed to an eight-hour workday. They would work for a while and then stop and not start again until he came by to check on them. Diebold appealed to the chief, who laid down the law and convinced them to work more consistently.

On the third day, pilot Davis arrived with their supplies and money. They got everything they'd asked for except the shovels. Diebold learned to his dismay that there were no shovels in India! Fortunately, the men were able to dig up and cut the roots of the smaller stumps with the pickaxes and axes. But the larger ones had to be blasted away using dynamite. This part made Diebold a bit uneasy because he had never used dynamite before. Davis quickly dropped a set of instructions to be followed to the letter. The dynamite caps had to be handled carefully. Just the heat from a hand could set them off. "To say that we handled them gingerly would be an understatement," wrote Diebold.

"WE DIDN'T BREATHE WHEN THE BOX WAS OPENED."

Diebold and Brenner began to put together their first charge of dynamite. They attached a 6-inch fuse to the cap and then put the cap in a hole in the can of dynamite. Then they pulled the handle of the lighter, which automatically lit the fuse, and ran for cover. The instructions said that it took one minute to burn each inch of fuse. That meant the charge should go off in six minutes. Six minutes came and went, and there was no explosion. They waited. Ten minutes passed. Then fifteen. What was wrong?

The two men crept back to the stump where the dynamite was set. The lighter hadn't lit the fuse, so they tried again. This time the fuse lit properly, and the dynamite went off as planned.

But when they returned to the stump, it was still there. All the dynamite had done was blow a hole in the earth around the thick roots of the stump. Diebold discovered that placing another can of dynamite under the exposed roots would tear the roots apart and allow the stump to be removed. One by one, the big stumps disappeared. After days of hard labor and dynamite explosions, the field was finally clear. But at 850 feet in length, would it be long enough for a plane to take off and land?

THE FINAL TEST

The next day, a small two-seater ambulance plane circled the field. Beside it were larger planes with official observers and military cameramen. It seemed that everyone wanted to see if Diebold's little airstrip in the jungle was going to work. As the small ambulance plane began its descent, the Americans stood watching, their hearts beating in their throats. Down, down, down the plane glided, landing perfectly on the airstrip and coming to a halt about halfway down the runway. Five hundred curious natives crowded around the plane while the Americans strapped Jacobs into the cabin. The takeoff was a bit trickier than the landing, but the plane easily cleared the trees as it soared into the sky.

Moments later, a second light plane came in for a landing. Brenner and Diebold insisted that Dr. Lamberts be the next passenger. This time the takeoff was considerably shakier, and the plane cleared the trees with just inches to spare. Brenner and Diebold decided that to avoid putting either pilot's life at risk a second time, they would depart the village on foot.

It was a grueling trek over the mountains. After five days, they arrived at the tea plantation. From there, they were picked up by a C-47 and transported back to their base in Mohanbari.

Back at base, the two men were ready for a little rest and recreation. But soon after they returned, Major Hedrick arrived at their tent. "Nice work," he said. "You did a good job. Be ready in the morning to go again; Captain Green just cracked up in Burma."

THE GRANDDADDY OF ALL STORMS

Friday, January 5, 1945, started off as just another day on the Hump. The early weather reports for outgoing flights were good. But as the day wore on, pilots returning to Assam told those going out that it was "pretty bad over the Hump." Then again, most days the weather was "pretty bad," and pilots didn't think much of it. However, once they flew into a storm that blanketed the Hump region, they thought differently.

But this was no ordinary storm. In fact, it would go down as the worst in the history of the Air Transport Command. The grim event would be forever known as "Black Friday."

What brought about what some have called the "granddaddy of all storms"? As with most turbulent weather, it was the result of the clash of hot and cold air masses. Cold air sweeping down from Siberia and warm air from the Bay of Bengal collided smack in the middle of the Himalayas, where the air was already cold. The result was a storm of monstrous proportions with tremendous winds, swirling snow, and pelting rain, hail, and sleet.

TEMPEST TOSSED

The crews that survived the storm each had their own story to tell. Pilot Robert H. Nicholas was flying a C-87 plane from Kunming to Tezpur on that fateful afternoon. He saw the storm dead ahead and tried to fly around it, but it proved too big for that. A terrible updraft lifted his plane upward like a toy at 3,000 feet per minute. The wind finally released its icy grip at 32,000 feet—the highest Nicholas had ever flown. Unlike some pilots, Nicholas made it safely to Tezpur, but his plane was running on fumes.

"Everything was so bright and clear, with Mount Liki sparkling to the north and the [snow] ahead and to the south."

—PILOT ROBERT H. NICHOLAS RECALLING HIS EXPERIENCE ON "BLACK FRIDAY"

In contrast to the updraft Nicholas' experienced, a strong downdraft dropped Lieutenant Thomas M. Sykes' plane to the dangerously low altitude of 14,000 feet, which just cleared the mountaintops. Remembering the plane twisting on its side, Sykes later recalled, "we were on our backs, blown skyward like a leaf in a wind … hanging on the safety belt with dirt from the floor falling all around."

Finally when the winds subsided, he was able to regain control of the aircraft and fly to Assam. Several of the 23 drums of fuel on board had come loose and struck the plane's ceiling, but remarkably they did not break open and caused no damage.

Pilot Don Downie and his crew, who left their base around nightfall, experienced a more hazardous flight. Once they were in the air, the temperature took a nosedive. Ice buildup on the wings and propellers threatened to bring the plane down. With the compass needle spinning wildly, Downie and his crew lost all sense of direction. Through a cloud of static over the radio, they heard other pilots crying out "Mayday! Mayday!"—the international distress signal.

Downie managed to put the plane back on route and headed toward Kunming. But the pressure the entire crew was under took its toll. Copilot Bill Hanahan recalled,

> **"WE WERE WRINGING WET [WITH SWEAT] EVEN THOUGH THE COCKPIT WAS COLD AND THE OUTSIDE TEMPERATURE WAS MINUS 20."**

VICTIMS OF "BLACK FRIDAY"

Downie and his crew landed safely at Kunming and then started back for Chabua, braving the storm again. Once in the air they learned that all flights over the Hump had been canceled due to the storm. Had they known of the cancellations before they took off, they could have spent the night safe and warm in Kunming.

Downie and his crew made it safely back to their base, but others were not as lucky. The final toll from the two-day storm was grim. The official count was 14 planes lost, half of them ATC planes carrying 31 crewmen and passengers, all who died.

Despite the loss of life, some good did come out of this awful tragedy. Soon after, new rules were passed allowing pilots to delay their flights due to weather conditions. And only experienced pilots with more than 1,000 hours of flight time were allowed to carry passengers.

While the Black Friday storm was raging, the far larger storm of war was starting to wind down. Although the brave Hump airmen didn't realize it, their days flying this dangerous route were numbered.

LAST DAYS ON
THE HUMP

As the fierce winter of 1944–1945 gave way to spring, the Japanese were losing ground. American and British troops had already driven them out of Burma and many of the islands in the South Pacific. But defeat only made the Japanese troops fight all the harder, especially in China, one place where they refused to budge. Between late January and March 1945, several Chinese cities that were home to U.S. Air Force bases all fell to the Japanese.

THE FINAL SURGE

Hump planes were now carrying thousands of American troops over the mountains to fight the Japanese and save China from collapse. Meanwhile in Europe, Japan's ally Germany was crumbling. Driven out of France, the Germans were fighting desperately to keep the Allies from overrunning their homeland. But they could not hold the Allied forces back. On April 30 Nazi leader Adolf Hitler took his own life rather than face capture and defeat. A week later, on May 7, Germany surrendered. The war in Europe was over, but the conflict in Asia and the Pacific continued.

As a result, Hump operations went into overdrive. During the month of July, Hump airmen set a record by delivering 71,042 tons of supplies to China. General Tunner was determined to keep the supplies flowing, and no one was going to stop him, not even his superiors. When Air Force Commander General Henry "Hap" Arnold ordered all commands to celebrate Air Force Day on August 1, Tunner ignored the order. Instead he pushed his airmen to break the record for the number of missions in one day.

They reached this goal, flying 1,118 flights over the Hump that day. Hump airmen delivered 5,327 tons of supplies—nearly 4 tons per minute.

SURRENDER AND CELEBRATION

Days earlier, Japan refused an ultimatum to surrender issued by the United States. On August 6, 1945, an American plane dropped a new and terrible weapon—the atomic bomb—on the Japanese city of Hiroshima. Despite the mass devastation this caused, the Japanese still refused to surrender. The Americans then dropped a second atomic bomb on the city of Nagasaki. An estimated 130,000 died instantly in the two cities with many more injured. Five days later, on August 14, the Japanese finally surrendered. The long war was over.

Perhaps no American servicemen were more stunned by the news than the Hump airmen in the CBI. Far from the main theaters of war, they knew nothing of atomic bombs and nuclear weapons. The idea that the Japanese—such a powerful enemy for so long—had surrendered was almost unbelievable.

That night as the news sunk in, there were no planes on the runways waiting to take off. The airmen celebrated.

"… for the first time since 1942, there was no sound of aircraft engines being 'run-up' for the day's flying. The silence was eerie and wonderful!"
—Pilot Otha C. Spencer

The war had ended, but the work of the Hump airmen continued. Tens of thousands of American airmen and soldiers were still stationed across China. Getting them out would take time, and until then, they still needed food and other supplies. That August, 53,315 tons of materials were flown into China. At the same time, Chinese troops had to be flown from their current bases into areas of the vast country previously occupied by Japan. By the start of November, more than 100,000 Chinese soldiers had been transported to such formerly occupied cities as Shanghai and Nanking. That month the figure for supplies sent dropped to 1,429 tons. The Hump airlift was nearing its end.

A SECOND WAR

Yet as one war was ending, a second one was heating up. From their headquarters in the north, Chinese Communists led by Mao Zedong began an intensive attack on the Nationalist forces of Chiang Kai-shek. The Nationalist government, which was riddled with corruption, had been weakened by the war.

The Americans were ready to go home, but they did what they could to support the Nationalist Chinese against the Communists. They gave some of the planes to the Nationalists and destroyed others so they couldn't be used by the Communists. Both fighter and transport planes were cut up for scrap metal. For the Hump pilots, watching their beloved planes destroyed was an emotional experience.

But the airmen still had a job to do—flying American troops out of China to catch flights home. However, this time the route would not be west over the Himalayas to India, but east across China to the Pacific.

No one wanted to be among the last Americans lost on the Hump.

But the dying was not quite over. In November three squadrons of the 14th Air Force flew to Calcutta from Shanghai. Two of the three squadrons made it safely back to Shanghai. The third did not. Eleven planes and their crews were lost. What happened is not clear. They either became lost and crashed during a thunderstorm or missed the Chinese coast and plunged into the ocean. It was a sad ending to a heroic era.

For the rest of the Hump airmen, it was time to go home. Some were so anxious that they didn't wait for a flight but instead caught the slow and crowded Assam-Bengal train, known as the "Cannonball Express." Others caught flights to Karachi and waited there for larger planes to take them to the States. Some, like pilot Carl Constein, boarded ships in India for a three-week ocean voyage to New York City. Seasick, but in good spirits, Constein arrived there on December 7. The welcome he received as he stepped off the Staten Island Ferry into Manhattan was a memorable one.

"I heard music. There … was a Scottish bagpipe band, perhaps forty, piping their welcome. It was two in the morning. … I got goose bumps. Did they greet all troop ships, or was the fourth anniversary of Pearl Harbor a special occasion? It was one of those unexpected special joys that remain with you always."

—CARL CONSTEIN REMEMBERING THE WELCOME HE RECEIVED WHEN HE ARRIVED IN NEW YORK CITY

Many veterans of the CBI Theater took the longer sea route home to the United States.

JAPAN SURRENDERS

Japan's official surrender to the Allies took place nearly a month after the United States dropped atomic bombs on Hiroshima and Nagasaki. The solemn ceremony took place on the morning of Sunday, September 2, 1945, aboard the battleship U.S.S. *Missouri* in Tokyo Bay. More than 250 Allied warships lay at anchor around it.

General Douglas MacArthur, head of the Allied Occupation of Japan, gave a brief address. Then Japanese Foreign Minister Mamoru Shigemitsu signed two copies of the surrender papers in Japanese and English. When a Japanese general, representing the armed forces, signed, his aides wept. MacArthur signed for the United Nations and another 10 representatives of Allied nations signed as well. As the sun broke through the clouds, MacArthur ended the 20-minute ceremony with these words: "Let us pray that peace be now restored to the world, and that God will preserve it always."

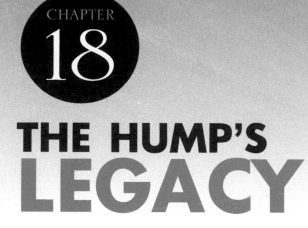

CHAPTER

18

THE HUMP'S
LEGACY

The Hump airlift of the CBI Theater unjustly remains one of the least-known events of World War II. And yet, without the efforts of these courageous pilots and crews, the war in the Pacific and Far East might have had a very different outcome. Perhaps British Prime Minister Winston Churchill said it best in a speech before the House of Commons in September 1944:

"This incredible feat of transport at … 22,000 feet in the air … when engine failure means certain death to the pilot, has been performed by a grand effort … Certainly no [greater] example of strength, science and organization in this class of work has ever been seen …"

In the mission's three years of existence, the Hump airmen delivered more than 700,000 tons of supplies to the Chinese front. Without this support China would have almost certainly fallen to the Japanese. This would have given the Japanese the means to continue the fight in the Pacific much longer, prolonging World War II, and potentially costing thousands of more lives on both sides. Instead, about a million Japanese troops were fighting in China and unable to fight the United States in the Pacific Theater.

THE SEARCH GOES ON

The price for the Hump's success, however, was a high one. More than 1,000 men died and nearly 600 planes were lost in the operation. The exact number of men lost and many of their fates remain unknown. For every survivor rescued in the jungles of Burma or the mountains of China and India, many more were found dead or never found at all. Government efforts to search and recover downed planes and their crews and passengers continued for a few years after the war ended. In recent years, private individuals—most notably Arizona businessman and adventurer Clayton Kuhles—have continued the search for the lost planes and airmen. In 2002 a native guide led Kuhles to a crashed C-47 in the mountains of north Burma. Since then Kuhles has made numerous trips to the region to search for planes and the remains of the men who flew them. As of 2012, he had visited 22 crash sites and found the remains of 193 people. He reports his findings to the U.S. Department of Defense and delivers any remains to them for DNA testing. Once identified, remains are returned to relatives of the deceased, if possible.

THE BERLIN AIRLIFT

There is another legacy of the Hump that lived on beyond the war it helped to end. As the first massive airlift of its kind, the Hump operation served as a blueprint for an even greater one, the Berlin airlift of 1948–1949. This monumental operation was directed by the same man who led the Hump in its final days, General William Tunner.

After World War II, the Soviet Union— the former ally of the United States—became the aggressor. The Soviet Union forced its Communist way of life onto a number of countries in Eastern Europe. It also occupied the eastern half of defeated Germany and its capital, Berlin. The United States, Great Britain, and France occupied the western part of Germany and Berlin. Hoping to drive the Allies out of the city and impose

Children of East Berlin watch as a plane prepares to drop food and supplies during the Berlin airlift of 1948–1949.

their own rule, the Soviets blockaded West Berlin in June 1948. To keep West Berliners from starving, the Allies dropped food and supplies into the city from planes.

The blockade was lifted in May 1949, but the airlift continued until the end of September. During that time, more than 2.3 million tons of food, medicine, and other supplies were delivered to West Berlin.

WEST BERLIN REMAINED A BEACON OF FREEDOM IN A REPRESSED LAND.

Without the Hump airlift, the Berlin airlift might never have happened.

The Hump airlift's legacy in China had a very different ending. The civil war between Chiang Kai-shek's Nationalists and Mao Zedong's Communists ramped up after World War II. The Communists eventually won out. Mao established the People's Republic of China, a Communist state, on October 1, 1949. Chiang Kai-shek, his troops, and his government were forced to flee to the island of Taiwan, about 100 miles off the coast of China. Today, Taiwan is considered a province of China but maintains its own government.

THE REST OF THE
STORY

What became of the Hump airmen?
After the war, many left the military and
returned to civilian life. Some remained
in the armed services, many serving bravely
in the Korean War (1950–1953). Others
became commercial pilots. Some of these
pilots put their knowledge and skills to

a group of airmen in Chengkung, China, in October 1944

work creating what came to be called the "golden age of air travel" in the 1950s and 1960s.

The following are the post-Hump stories of some of the airmen whose experiences were told in this book:

Lieutenant Carl Frey Constein (pilot) returned to college and eventually earned a doctorate from Temple University in Pennsylvania. He became a school superintendent and an educational writer. He wrote and edited several books about his war experiences and those of other Hump airmen.

Robert Crozier (pilot) returned to Baylor College after the war to earn his degree. He went on to become a vice president of the Texas Retail Grocers Association.

First Lieutenant William Diebold (search and rescue) found it difficult to adjust to civilian life after the war. His written account of his experiences on the Hump gathered dust in an attic for nearly 50 years after his death in 1965 at age 47. It was finally published in 2013.

First Lieutenant Robert A. Engels (copilot) became co-owner with his father of the Silver Dollar Bar in Ghent, Minnesota. He later moved with his family to Brookings, Oregon.

Private John Huffman (base mechanic) continued to be pursued by bad luck. He was injured in a plane crash in Europe before returning to the States. He never flew in an airplane again. Huffman became an engineer for Boeing Aircraft Company in Seattle, Washington, and later took up commercial fishing in Florida.

Technical Sergeant Marvin Jacobs recovered from his ordeal in an Indian hospital. After his discharge from the service, he returned to his hometown of Buffalo, New York.

Harold McCallum (pilot) met an American nurse in India, married her, and had five children. He became a corporate pilot for *Time* magazine's cofounder and president Henry Luce and later flew for the very wealthy Astor family.

Private First Class William Perram (flight engineer) died in a plane crash on another Hump mission just two months after returning from his adventure in Tibet. He was 23 years old.

Sergeant Walter Oswalt (radio operator) returned safely from the August 1943 C-46 crash in northern Burma. However, he died later that year on December 10, when the C-47 transport plane he was aboard was attacked by the Japanese and crashed.

Eric Sevareid (war correspondent) continued as a leading news correspondent for CBS after the war until 1977. After that he became a well-known commentator on CBS until his retirement in 1991.

Corporal Kenneth Spencer (radio operator) went to college and earned a degree in economics. He later became an administrator for Long Island Public Schools.

Otha C. Spencer (pilot) became a professor of journalism and photography at East Texas State University. He wrote hundreds of magazine articles and several books, including a comprehensive history of the Hump.

In an article about the Hump airmen, journalist Eric Sevareid summed up the achievement of these brave pilots in peril:

"WE HAVE A LONG LIST
OF UNSUNG HEROES IN THIS WAR,
AND THE AIR TRANSPORT COMMAND
YOUNGSTERS WHO HAVE FLOWN
THE HUMP DAY IN AND DAY OUT
OUGHT TO BE PLACED
NEAR THE HEAD OF THIS LIST."

TIMELINE

1894–1895
The First Sino-Japanese War ends with Japan defeating China. Japan occupies the island of Taiwan.

1931
Japan seizes the northern Chinese region of Manchuria.

1937
Japan invades China's eastern seaboard and closes its ports.

SEPTEMBER 3, 1939
Great Britain and France declare war on Germany after it invades Poland, signaling the start of War World II.

DECEMBER 7, 1941
Japan attacks the American naval fleet at Pearl Harbor, Hawaii. The next day the U.S. declares war on Japan.

APRIL 8, 1942
As part of the 10th Air Force, the first Hump flight (originally known as the Assam-Burma-China Command) leaves India to deliver war supplies to China.

MAY 1942
Burma falls to the Japanese.

DECEMBER 1, 1942
The Air Transport Command (ATC) takes over operation of the Hump route.

NOVEMBER 30, 1943
Robert Crozier, William Perram, John Huffman, Kenneth Spencer, and Harold McCallum get caught in a storm over the Hump while returning to their base in Jorhat, India. They bail out over Tibet and with the help of the natives begin a long journey back to their base.

JANUARY 20, 1944
After 51 days of exhausting travel through Tibet, pilot Crozier and his crew return safely to their base in Jorhat.

MARCH 29, 1944
American airmen Charles Allison, Robert Engels, Rocco Commaratto, and Edward Salay bail out of their aircraft as it plunges into a Chinese valley.

JULY 1, 1944
With help from a family of missionaries, Allison and his crew return safely to their base.

JULY 29, 1944
Lieutenant Greenlaw Collins parachutes into a jungle in Burma.

AUGUST 22, 1944
Hump airmen set a record for tonnage and flights made.

JANUARY 5–6, 1945
A monster storm takes the lives of 31 crew and passengers on the Hump.

JANUARY 12, 1945
The first convoy of troops heads to China on the Ledo Road. Built by American and Indian laborers, the Ledo Road provides a new land route to China.

FEBRUARY 3, 1945
Technical Sergeant Marvin Jacobs, sole survivor of a Hump plane crash, is stranded in an Indian jungle. He is later rescued by Lieutenant William Diebold.

MAY 7, 1945
Germany surrenders to the Allies. The war in Europe ends.

AUGUST 6 & 9, 1945
The United States drops two atomic bombs on the Japanese cities of Hiroshima and Nagasaki.

AUGUST 14, 1945
The Japanese surrender, ending the war in the East.

NOVEMBER 1945
The Hump airlift shuts down.

GLOSSARY

amputate—to cut off an arm, leg, or other body part

carburetor—the part of an engine that mixes oxygen with fuel before it is forced into the engine cylinders

convoy—group of vehicles traveling together

correspondent—one who contributes news to a newspaper or newscast often from a distant place

corruption—willingness to do things that are wrong or illegal to get money, favors, or power

crevice—a narrow opening or crack in a hard surface

disciplinarian—one who is very strict

dysentery—a serious and often deadly infection of the intestines caused by drinking contaminated water.

embassy—a building in one country where the representatives of another country work

gawk—to stare at something in a rude or stupid way

kamikaze—a Japanese pilot who purposely crashes his plane into a target, resulting in his own death

morale—a person or group's feelings or state of mind about a job or task

Nazi—a member of a political party led by Adolf Hitler; the Nazis ruled Germany from 1933 to 1945.

parapack—a package with a parachute attached so it can be dropped from an aircraft

pass—a low place in a mountain range

plasma—the liquid part of the blood that carries red blood cells, white blood cells, and platelets

puppet state—a conquered country whose leader is under the complete control of the conquering nation

sabotage—damage or destruction of property that is done on purpose

slipstream—an area of low air pressure immediately behind a vehicle that is moving very fast that other vehicles can ride to go faster with less effort

swastika—a cross with bent arms used to represent the German Nazi party

theater—an area or region where military operations take place in a war

trek—a slow, difficult journey

updraft—an upward movement of air

FURTHER READING

Burgan, Michael. *World War II Pilots: An Interactive History Adventure.* You Choose. North Mankato, Minn.: Capstone Press: 2013.

Darman, Peter. *Attack on Pearl Harbor: America Enters World War II.* New York: Rosen Publishing, 2013.

George, Enzo. *World War II in the Pacific: War with Japan.* Voices of War. New York: Cavendish Square Publishing, 2014.

Stein, R. Conrad. *World War II in the Pacific: From Pearl Harbor to Nagasaki.* Berkeley Heights, N.J.: Enslow Publishers, 2011.

CRITICAL THINKING USING THE COMMON CORE

1. Why was the Hump Operation so critical in the fight against Japan? (Key Ideas and Details)

2. What perils did the Hump airmen face that made their flight route one of the most treacherous in the entire war? (Craft and Structure)

3. What qualities did Lieutenant William Diebold have that made him such a successful member of the search-and-rescue squadron? (Integration of Knowledge and Ideas)

SELECT BIBLIOGRAPHY

Constein, Dr. Carl Frey. *Born to Fly … The Hump: The First Airlift.* Bloomington, Ind.: 1st Books, 2001.

Constein, Dr. Carl Frey, editor. *Tales of the Himalayas: Letters from WWII Airmen Who Flew the Hump.* Bloomington, Ind.: 1st Books, 2002.

Diebold, Lieutenant William. *Hell Is So Green: Search and Rescue Over The Hump in World War II.* Guilford, Conn.: Lyons Press, 2012.

Moser, Don. *China-Burma-India (World War II).* Alexandria, Va.: Time-Life Books, 1978.

Plating, John D. *The Hump: America's Strategy for Keeping China in World War II.* College Station: Texas A & M University Press, 2011.

Spencer, Otha C. *Flying the Hump: Memories of an Air War.* College Station: Texas A & M University Press, 1992.

Starks, Richard, and Miriam Murcutt. *Lost in Tibet: The Untold Story of Five American Airmen, a Doomed Plane, and the Will to Survive.* Guilford, Conn.: Lyons Press, 2004.

Sunderman, Major James F., ed. *World War II in the Air.* New York: Franklin Watts, 1962.

Underbrink, Robert. *Somewhere We Will Find You: Search and Rescue Operations in the CBI, 1942–1945.* Bennington, Vt.: Merriam Press, 2010.

SOURCE NOTES

Page 27, line 7: Otha C. Spencer. *Flying the Hump*. College Station:
Texas A & M University Press, 1992, p. 52.

Page 32, lines 7, 10, 13, and callout quote: Richard Starks and Miriam Murcutt.
Lost in Tibet. Guilford, Conn.: Lyons Press, 2004, p. 40.

Page 50, line 9: *Lost in Tibet*. p. 175.

Page 76, callout quotes: Robert Underbrink. *Somewhere We Will Find You*.
Bennington, Vt.: Merriam Press, 2010, p. 49.

Page 81, callout quote: *Flying the Hump*. p. 84.

Page 85, callout quote: *Somewhere We Will Find You*. p. 64.

Page 86, callout quote: Major James F. Sunderman, ed. *World War II in the Air*.
New York: Franklin Watts, 1962, p. 144.

Page 91, line 1: Don Moser. *China-Burma-India (World War II)*.
Alexandria, Va.: Time-Life Books, 1978. p. 84.

Page 94, callout quote: *Flying the Hump*. pp. 5, 6.

Page 95, line 11: Carl Constein. *Born to Fly ... The Hump*. Bloomington,
Ind.: 1st Books, 2001. p. 44.

Page 97, callout quote and line 12: *Born to Fly ... The Hump*. p. 124.

Page 98, line 4, ibid, p. 129.

Page 105, letter: *Somewhere We Will Find You*. p. 99.

Page 106, letter: ibid, p. 101.

Page 114, callout quote: *World War II in the Air*. p. 141.

Page 115, callout quote: Carl Constein. *Tales of the Himalayas*.
Bloomington, Ind.: 1st Books, 2002. p. 157.

Page 119, callout quote: *Flying the Hump*. p. 167.

Page 120, line 10: ibid, p. 168.

Page 123, callout quote: *Born to Fly ... The Hump*. p. 79.

Page 132, lines 4, 7, and callout quote: Ellayne Conyers. "Letter from a WWII
Soldier (Part III)," http://marshallindependent.com/page/content.detail/
id/557524/Letter-from-a-WWII-soldier--Part-III-.html?nav=5007.
Retrieved October 2, 2014.

Page 135, callout quote: ibid.

Page 139, line 7: General William H. Tunner. *Over the Hump*. New York:
Duell, Sloan and Pearce, 1964, p. 88.

Page 152, letter: *Somewhere We Will Find You*. p. 75.

Page 153, callout quote: William Diebold. *Hell Is So Green*. Guilford, Conn.: Lyons Press, 2012, p. 55.

Page 157, line 14: ibid, p. 6.

Page 159, callout quote: ibid, p. 17.

Page 161, callout quotes: ibid, pp. 26, 43.

Page 168, line 3 and callout quote: ibid, p. 79.

Page 168, line 15: ibid, p. 80.

Page 170, callout quote: ibid, p. 83.

Page 177, line 2: ibid, p. 206.

Page 182, line 3 and callout quote: ibid, pp. 233–234.

Page 185, line 17: ibid, p. 253.

Page 188, line 18: *Tales of the Himalayas*. p. 153.

Page 190, callout quote: *Flying the Hump*. p. 157.

Page 190, line 9: ibid, p. 156.

Page 192, callout quote: *Born to Fly ... The Hump*. p. 127.

Page 199, callout quote: *Flying the Hump*. p. 171.

Page 203, callout quote: *Born to Fly ... The Hump*. pp. 133–134.

Page 208, callout quote: "Critical Problems of Past, Present and Future: Review of Military and Political Situations." Winston Churchill.
Delivered in the House of Commons, London, September 28, 1944.
http://www.ibiblio.org/pha/policy/1944/1944-09-28a.html.
Retrieved April 2, 2015.

Page 223, callout quote: *World War II in the Air,* p. 141.

INDEX

ABOUT THE AUTHOR

Steven Otfinoski has written more than 170 books for young readers. His many books include U.S. Army True Stories: Tales of Bravery; World War II Infantrymen: An Interactive History Adventure; and The Sinking of the Lusitania: An Interactive History Adventure.